T0343592

GAZ'S ROCKIN BOOK

GAZ MAYALL

TROLLEY

GAZ'S ROCKIN' BLUES

EVERY THURSDAY
FREE MEMBERSHIP

69, DEAN
(CORNER OF

OPENING NIGHT

THU JULY 3rd

REGGAE
&
BLUES
DANCE

ROCKIN' SOUNDS

D.J. GAZ plus friends

W.1.

RD ST)

ADMISSION   £2

LICENCED FROM 9 – 3 a.m.

I DEDICATE THIS BOOK TO
MIN LILLA ÄLSKLING ELINOR FAHRMAN
WHOSE INVALUABLE HELP MADE
THIS BOOK HAPPEN.

Gaz Mayall behind
his flat on Harrow
Road, 1991

THE BEGINNING

The party really started a year earlier in the spring of 1979. Congregating in the youth culture playground of Kensington Market, hundreds followed by thousands of young people into alternative fashion and music descended on the stalls, shops, cafés and pool halls of the giant indoor clothes emporium on Kensington High Street. It was situated roughly a mile south of the epicentre of the heartland of my world, Portobello Market, and only a short walk through the park (Ken Gardens) from my basement in Orme Square on the Bayswater Road. Significantly it was less than half a mile from Holland Park School, which I'd attended somewhat intermittently in the early 70's since moving to the area from South East London in 1970.

Ken Market had risen to prominence during the 60's as a minor citadel of fashion to rival the indoor clothes market of King's Road, specialising in cheap handmade garments, shoes and bags. Along with Biba down the road it was one of our favourite local haunts to go and eye up, with a mind to steal clothes we couldn't afford, while truanting from our nearby school. By the late 70's the place had deteriorated badly. Up to two thirds of the stalls were boarded up or in the process of closing down. The majority of those that remained were totally out of step with current fashion. Mainly run by Asians still trying to flog naff, stack-soled, high-heeled, snakeskin boots and tight-fitting leather gear, they were reminiscent of Gary Glitter, heavy rock and the longhaired hippie era of years ago. Paint peeled from walls and ceilings and damp crept about all three floors from the basement up. On the first floor, Turks ran the large pool hall at the back and the smaller one incorporating the café at the front, above the bank on the corner. The Turks up there tended to be short-tempered, standoffish, belligerent and suspicious. Quick to snap, bark and bite, with pool queues coming into play during the occasional fight. The pool hall and café seemed a charade and haven for heroin dealings, judging by the amount of junkies skulking about collecting their wraps. The whole market appeared seedy and in decline. I'd just spent a few years in mid-Wales, antique dealing on and off with my mother. I was 20 years old, libido on fire, girl crazy and having committed myself to a life of self-employment, I returned home to take my chances in West London. It was the autumn of '78.

I arrived back sniffing around, looking for a niche and a way to make a living. I popped into Ken Market to see an old girlfriend, Sophie, who'd been running her stall there on the first floor for a few months selling second-hand girls clothes. She was turning over around £70 a week. Her overheads and stock were costing her very little and my mind was clicking away like an overheated pocket calculator. Next door to hers was Avril doing a similar thing but more stylishly, more new-wave, more stilettos, handbags and fishnets. Opposite Avril's, backing on to the Turkish café, was Ian. A short, young, amiable, South African, gay guy whose immaculately laid out little glass fronted shop also ventured into menswear. It was a happy, buzzing little corner of an otherwise seemingly dying market. An almost empty warren of clothes shops, whose saving grace and lifeline was the popular 'Johnson and Johnson's' on the far side of the same floor, famous for their great shoes, shirts and suits modelled on the 50's vivid, pink and black and flecked outfits, they were suited to the slick tastes of fashionistas into punk and new wave, as well as the strictly 50's rock'n'roll aficionados.

Sophie introduced me to Colin, the moustached manager, responsible for filling the empty stalls, eager to resuscitate the market and get people back in. I was nearly penniless so had to take the smallest and cheapest spot he had to offer, a tiny stall next to the pool hall, close to Avril's for £40 a month. It was opposite a black guy called Fritz, who was selling mainly reggae records and some R&B and rockabilly albums he had on sale or return. I went in halves with a slightly older friend, Simon Lee, a part-time teacher with a penchant for loud colours, who was weaning himself off a smack habit and dabbling in methadone. Not the most reliable or ideal partner, he soon slid by the wayside, leaving me ticking by alone with the clothes and paraphernalia I was picking up cheaply from markets, clearing out from home or was donated by friends doing the same.

We closed for a short Christmas break, returning to find Fritz's record shop burgled and all but cleared out of what little stock he had on tick. He asked me for help as I got on very well with Colin and his side-kick rent collector Basil. Colin accepted no responsibility and afforded no financial compensation, but out of sympathy he offered the pair of us a premises immediately opposite Sophie's, which by comparison to the meagre sizes of our stalls seemed huge. It overlooked the high street from its large windows, the height and width of the shop. The space was large - stout and oblong with a high ceiling and a fabulous arched entrance, with a stream of light bulbs fitted to the front of the arch, illuminating the passage for passers-by. It had solid walls, wooden floorboards, Victorian embellishments, some shelving and most favourably, to top it all, metal shutters at the entrance, which rolled down to padlock to the floor.

A Chinese guy was due to vacate it and it could be ours within a couple of weeks. Taking a hot tip piece of advice from Ian, I went to Colin's office to strike a deal. I gave him an envelope of £50 for himself and a bottle of brandy for Basil and asked for his very best price. We settled at a very friendly £45 per week with no deposit. As long as we paid promptly each week he'd keep the rate at that indefinitely with no hikes. I borrowed £200 cash off my mother's best friend Malcolm, and ended up paying him back within six weeks. We decorated and stocked it and were up and running in no time. The first week we were open I sold over £70 worth of stock that had cost me a fiver. Fritz sold one LP for four quid. He realised it was going to be a dead loss so I bought him out and he left after the second week, which had similarly proved to be no better for him.

My stepfather, Geoff Wynn, an artist and sign-writer by trade, came down from Wales and painted a sandwich board which I placed daily on the street outside the main entrance. It read 'Upstairs GAZ clothes and records'. He also painted in red, yellow and green, three large letters 'GAZ' to adorn the big window inside. I'd needed a simple nickname for my shop as all the other people's stalls were referred to by their names. Gary sounded wrong and had no pizzazz, and Geoff in typical northern fashion had often called me Gaz the Waz. My old friend Damian, a sound engineer and son of my mentor, DJ and blues musician Alexis Korner, came in and hooked up a sound system. I brought in more shop fittings, found cheap or picked up off the street. I moved in loads of 45 singles from my large record collection that I'd gathered through recent years. Lots of 60's soul, ska, reggae and rock'n'roll. I stocked the place up with loads of cool, old, second-hand and unworn end of line original 20's through to 60's gents clothing and spread the word. Cleaned, pressed and shoes shined, the scene was set for what proved to be one long, hot, crazed, almighty, non-stop party. It provided the backdrop for one and a half years until I quit and moved the action and people base to my new club 'Gaz's Rockin' Blues'.

As it had been in my school days six or seven years back, there was no school uniform at Holland Park Comprehensive and the school gates were left open throughout the day. The temptation to bunk off was too great and now wandering pupils created a new influx of wayward kids. I thought the least I could do was give them a place to hang out and learn something about different genres of music and fashion. I'd be up with the dawn and down the 'Bella Friday and Saturday mornings and back to open the shop by 10am. On Sundays I was at Brick Lane at 4am befriending all the right stallholders, who I got to save me all their best gear. I was after the finest two-tone mohair tonic suits, Brutus trim-fit shirts, loafers, brogues and 60's mod and skinhead clothes that had been denied me as a kid. By early '79 I was wearing the cream of the crop of all the tastiest clothes I'd ever wanted. While the high street had little or nothing to offer, I was bringing in bales of 40's, 50's and 60's hats, shirts and teddy boy drapes and ties. I had good leads on nylon-striped socks from New York, every colour of half-inch braces, leather rockers, jackets and PVC biker suits. GAZ became an Aladdin's cave of every rebel youth culture revolution since the war. The local lads lapped it up trying on every style for size and we had the soundtrack to go with it. Music blaring out all day long. Saturday was the big day. Within a couple of months of the opening, our corner of the market was heaving with young people, not just shopping but on a social adventure to hang, chat, meet, flirt, chill and party all day long. Kids soon arrived from East, North and South London as word spread that it was the best place to get all this, the clothes being a fraction the price of off-the-peg new.

By spring some of the regular lads seemed to spend the greater part of the whole week in and around my shop. Byron Upton, from an artistic family who were best friends with David Hockney, was only fourteen but already the life and soul of the party. He lived locally in Colville Square, just around the corner from the Electric Cinema. His mother Anne happily encouraged him hanging out with us. Byron introduced lots of like minded kids from Pimlico where he went to school, including Eddie Harman, who would later become my right hand DJ Rock Steady Eddie for fifteen years. He also introduced black rudy Johnny T. JT was big on reggae, played violin and had great stories about anti-fascist demos he'd been on. There was the Clapham set, with Morgan Jackson and Co, Christian Coral from Chelsea, local boys Josh Ritchie, Spanish Luis and a snappy blue/black tonic mohair suited Big John Thompson, who always lit the place up with his big personality and smile to match his size.

There was also Dom Bajic, a Bradford born lad who hadn't lost his northern accent as I had since arriving from Manchester as a boy. He lived in a gated community facing Hyde Park, just up the road from me. We hung out all the time like long lost brothers. He and his best friend Hans used to change styles every few months. One week they'd be total skinheads, the next punks, then rockabillys, rudies or whatever took them.

I was now 21. Most of the kids hanging out were on average five or six years younger. I was the eldest of five boys with one sister. Jason, a year and a half younger, was living with my dad in LA and only returning during the summer and for Christmas. Ben, my next brother, jet-black and adopted from birth, boarded at his school in Bredon near Tewkes-bury. When he came back at half-term, aged fourteen and very tall with it, we kitted him out with all the best clothes he fancied – from a pork pie hat down to his Dr Martens boots. He was instantly popular and part of the scene, making lots of new friends and spending most of his free time in the market with us.

Another significant factor in the rise and renewal of Ken Market's reputation, that massively boosted its numbers and put it firmly back on the London map, was the closure of Beaufort Market in the World's End of King's Road. It had been a bastion of cult fashion for the past few years and was due to close its doors for good by April Fool's Day to make way for a new posh shopping mall. Beaufort Market was situated close to Malcolm MacLaren and Vivienne Westwood's shop 'Sex' and between them they'd kick started the whole punk rock movement. The stalls there, during the punk years of '76 – '78 had been the heart and home of punk fashion, a creative source, home and birthplace to a myriad of bands and clothes designers. Poly Styrene formed X-Ray Spex there and had her stall/shop selling clothes made from black plastic bin liners. Jock McDonald of The Bollock Brothers would preach punk rhetoric from his soap box there. Running battles with punks, teds and police were common all along that section of the street.

With its closure there was only one obvious place for all the shop and stall owners to relocate to - Ken Market. So you can imagine the upheaval and the ensuing chaotic rush to get the best pitches. Every floor started filling up fast, every site that was up for grabs was grabbed, shaken and revolutionised. With the introduction of hoards of extra punks it became one explosively creative summer.

In May '79 The Specials hit the news. All of a sudden for the first time a band had made headlines with our favourite brand of music - ska. They were all over the NME and Melody Maker, the two most prominent music papers of the day, sporting the kind of second-hand clothes we were all wearing that were featured in my shop. They went straight to number one of the charts with 'Gangsters', a version of Prince Buster's 'Al Capone', the original of which we'd been playing regularly at the shop. Along with the onslaught of new punters and young entrepreneurs came James Lebon, a Jewish lad I'd known along with his older brother, photographer Mark, for some time. He set up a hairdressers in the basement, called 'James Cuts'. Now all our crew had cheap or complimentary haircuts to go with our cool outfits. My place was getting so busy, especially on Saturdays that I was beginning to need help. There was a dark side to the market's booming popularity, thieving. There was one gang in particular to watch out for, the LGS – the Ladbroke Grove Skins, run by fruit and veg barrow boy Chris Harwood. Chris was jovial and we always got on fine, but some of the others would try and have something away if you weren't sharp enough.

So with this in mind, while strolling one afternoon through Notting Hill Gate towards the 'Bella, I passed the old shop in Pembridge Road where I'd had my very first stall, aged fifteen, outside a second-hand clothes shop run by an elderly Jewish couple, Mr and Mrs Philips. They'd specialised in old riding boots, and it was there I'd bought my first pair of spats, my first pinstriped suit, my first wide-brimmed Stetson hat and got my first taste and knowledge for the trade I was now in. Lo and behold, guess who I should see but Lance Jowers. I hadn't seen him since he'd last visited our house in Southbrook Road, Lee Green, ten years ago, when we got in loads of trouble with his mum. He'd pinched a few bob from her purse and we'd gone to the corner shop, where he'd bought a penknife. She marched us back to the shop and made them take it back. We can't have been more than eleven years old. He had such a distinctive and unforgettable face, with a strong jaw-line, and here he was, bright-eyed, full of confidence and with the same jaw-line, swaggering along Pembridge Road, with a cool crew of tough-looking young characters, all of who had our look. I crossed the road and surprised him with a brief ten-year update and told him about the market. Within a fortnight we were best friends again and he was working every Saturday at my stall and he introduced his gang to the place. He was singing in a band called The Nobodiez, and his pals all had really cool names, like Mole, Bone and Meathead. I swear Meathead really didn't have a neck, just this square head attached straight to his thick shoulders.

Quadrophenia came out, adding hundreds of new kids to the menagerie, searching for new mod outfits along with the rude boys and skins influenced by the two-tone craze sweeping the nation. Unlike the King's Road rivalries between punks and teddy boys and the traditional enmity between mods and rockers, we all got on like one big mad, happy, weird sort of family. In fact the only real trouble seemed to come from the odd clash with the pool hall Turks, who didn't know what had hit them with this avalanche of crazy young kids. Lots of teenagers joined the ranks of stallholders. Seventeen-year-old Jessie Birdsall opened a great little record shop called Chicken Shack with his partners Mark Jamieson, selling 50's repro 45's, adding doo-wop and rockabilly to the catalogue of sounds streaming through the corridors. One of Beaufort Market's diaspora, Blues, set up shop on the ground floor. I couldn't quite understand why they only had half a dozen punk t-shirts up for sale, until I realised it was just a front for selling 'blues' – little blue pills better known as speed. Before you knew it the whole market was speeding its tits off.

With such an array of great things to choose from and such a good vibe Ken Market had never been so popular, at least not since its heyday in the 60's and probably not even then. The place was crowded every day. Famous musicians from all the top name bands would visit and peruse. Madness, The Clash and a host of artists you may or may not have heard of, popularised the place even more. Ken Market became so busy throughout the rest of '79 that Portobello Market was practically devoid of youngsters for nearly a year.

It was one afternoon in late summer and one of our regular pals, a quiet skinhead called Jim Hall, was rolling around on the floor with his girlfriend Lucy Mott, when Andrew Czezowski turned up for one of his little chats, about something else he was setting up. We always had people popping in for little chats, usually self-opinionated guys like Rusty Egan, bragging about their latest thing or about how crap so and so, or this and that is was. I liked having Jim around. He rarely spoke a word and kind of balanced out the egocentrics. He'd been a skinhead since he was a kid and kept the faith right the way through a stint through Borstal and young offenders. He never worked, and made a living instead working his magic on slot machines and cheating them out of their small change. So here by contrast arrives Andrew, the guy that started the Vortex Club, the premier punk club at the Roxy. He was starting a new club in Oxford Street in Studio 21, up by Tottenham Court Road tube station and would I like to come and DJ. It was to be called 'The Two-Tone Club', riding off the back of the ska and mod craze. He had the 60's pop and soul side covered and needed me to play the Jamaican rude boy tunes and obviously fill the club with my friends and clientele. He said he'd drop in some flyers and we opened in October.

THE TWO-TONE CLUB

The club had obviously had little make over since the 60's and was an ideal setting for a great night out for us. With raised seating areas around the dance floor, the DJ area, not much more than a ground-level table with chest-high boarding in front, was right at the back, which made for direct contact with the dancers, but was vulnerable to drink spillages when lairy revellers were leering over, pestering requests. It was for most of us our first taste of night-clubbing. There was no real issue with underage drinking in those days. Most fellas and girls from Ken Market were blatantly below the legal age of eighteen, everyone dressed up in predominantly 60's mod and rude boy fashion. Amongst our regular crew were plenty of slicked up skinheads including Lance, Dom, Jim and the like, aspiring to be like the immaculately turned out skins I remembered from school days, first time around. Andrew's concept of what he was aiming for with the night wasn't going down well enough with the majority of us as the music was far too cheesy. The corny retro music his DJs were playing was the kind of pop that was considered awfully commercial and had little or nothing to do with the two-tone sounds we'd thought we'd come to hear. I was hustled onto the decks with my two small colourful vinyl singles cases, each held about twenty or twenty-five records. I'd brought pretty much nothing but Jamaican ska, rocksteady and skinhead reggae. All original UK 45's that we'd been spinning daily down the market. The place went wild. No one would let me leave the decks until I'd completely exhausted my selection. We were like a huge bunch of kids at a massive dress up party, reliving an event we'd been cheated out of by being born too late. We felt empowered, come of age, finally getting our due - and we all looked fantastic.

The following week we were all down there again in full force. I carried a lot more tunes this time. I was given prime slot again, the vibes were great, drinks flowed, the dance floor was rammed and the place was jumping. Then out of nowhere calamity struck. A small group of out of place casuals, straight-looking geezers from St Albans who were cruising the West End, had just wandered in off the street. They had been hassling some of the girls and were drunk and kept leaning over the DJ decks, being annoying.

Jim somehow became their target, as he tried to help give me space so I could play undeterred, when bang, the whole place kicked off, fists and bottles flew, glasses and tables crashed. Jim was a great fighter but there were quite a few of them and he took the brunt. Big John mucked in as did Dom, Hans, Lou Banks and Lance. The bouncers soon came and restored order but the management pinpointed all the lads in skinhead attire and they became the scapegoats and were banned from the club from the following week. I did go back the next week but the club owners stuck to their guns. Jim arrived with a handful of his Chelsea firm, circling the West End in vain, searching for the St Albans thugs who'd vowed to return. A sizeable portion of our friends weren't allowed back in which we all thought draconian and wrong. Me and loads of our mutual disgruntled friends left and never returned. Without us the Two-Tone club pretty soon died a death but the fun we'd had in that short time was immense and we'd got ourselves a real taste of the nightlife we now craved. It was only a matter of time before we'd get back in to the West End on our own terms and get a proper footing.

We did go to some great concerts and saw bands like The Specials and some top reggae and blues artists at places such as Dingwalls and the 100 club. Gigs were expensive and most of our pals were either too young to work or were just plain skint. The hub of our social life was still the market. When that closed at six we would usually relocate to my place. A new bunch of girls that frequented the shop had recently formed a band called 'The Bodysnatchers'. We gave them a bit of support and followed them about for their first gigs at the Windsor Castle in Harrow Road and the Dublin Castle in Camden Town. They needed more original material so I dragged them all back to my place where I wrote 'We're Ruder Than You' for them with their singer Rhoda. I had an old white upright piano in my room and several other instruments knocking around and had for years been jamming the night away with my friends in that basement. One night the neighbours phoned at 2am complaining that we sounded like a train careering through their house. We weren't big drinkers but did smoke a lot of weed, or draw, as we preferred to call it for subtlety's sake.

I wasn't quite good enough yet to form a band, but was eager to spread the music and get more involved. What money I didn't plough back into my business, my stomach or the odd spliff, I'd spend on records. Buying collections by the box-load from Portobello Market and Brick Lane of any vintage stuff that appealed to me. It was amazing what would turn up. Some types of music, like soul, were so sought after and the prices so high, that I spent the bulk of what I had on music that tended to be overlooked, unnoticed and underground. Particularly Jamaican sounds kept turning up, of which I soon acquired a formidable collection. Reggae was one of the kinds of music I'd always followed and was still buying new releases as they came out. There was no shortage of record shops, shacks and stalls in the Grove, Camden Market and Hanwell Street in the West End. There was one stall in Camden, run by a guy called John, who regularly saved me Bluebeat singles that I'd been collecting since I was fourteen. His son, a big eyed ten year-old kid, was hatted, suited and booted with a black soul singer painted of the back of his parka. He was so enthusiastic and knowledgeable about the music, I promised him a job upon leaving school. He later became one of my top DJs, the great Count Cassavubu.

There were also huge record fairs where I could find original hardcore 50's black dance music on 45's that rarely showed up outside of Ted Carroll's Ace record shop, 'Rock On' in Camden. His record shack at the back of 93, Golborne Road up my way had been the single most important source of my R&B and rock'n'roll collection. I'd whiled away many a Saturday afternoon there prior to my Ken Market days. As we were closed Sundays, I'd spend most of them in Camden, including a few hours at his mothership there. He even had 78's of things I'd only ever seen on compilation LPs. Ted was always chatty and fun, in a dry acerbic sort of way, always imparting knowledge and opinions on a wide range of music. He had his own label, starting in the punk days with Chiswick Records, then Ace, named after the New Orleans R&B label he'd acquired the UK rights to. He continually kept pumping out great singles and albums of re-releases all new to us.

I kept some of the rarer R&B at home to air only to close friends or DJ at the odd party here and there. I was turning more space in the corner of my shop over to records. When the sound system faulted I moved in an old Dansette portable player. Friends kept the tunes spinning and minded the place while I toured the market visiting other stalls socialising, playing pool or out on buying trips. By Christmas '79 mine was among the most happening and most influential stalls in the market. One Saturday we took over a thousand pounds. Lance and I would get back to my flat after and empty out all our pockets, throwing piles of notes and change onto the bed. You could hardly see the bedspread for cash. We felt rich in every sense. A few days later Lance and friends had conspired to arrange a surprise birthday party in Orme Square for my 22nd. The whole gang was there. James Lebon, Sophie and other Ken Market stalwarts. Singers and musicians such as Dan-I and The Bodysnatchers, old school friends Mark Tuft and Co and my whole family back from Wales, Gloucestershire and America. I'd never been so popular.

THE END OF THE BEGINNING

        I kind of peaked at the tail end of the year and started the new decade with a little uphill climb against the wind and some emotional rain. I'd had a little dose of heartbreak and found myself quite shy and clumsy in my first few attempts at love. Girls did like me a lot but were more attracted to bigger shots, slicker talkers and better looking guys who were more comfortable with themselves where romance and sex was concerned. My time and thoughts were immersed in my business, my friends, music and trying to get somewhere in the world. Love being a major distraction, a hindrance to my work, I'd just fumbled and stumbled my way through another brief bout of it, starting the year dumped and miserable.

By Valentine's Day I picked myself up, dusted myself off and put my focus fully back into the scene. The clothes business wasn't suffering due to lack of drive or enthusiasm, but had become a victim of its own success. So many new stalls in Ken Market were doing the same lines as myself, as were other specialist second-hand and retro shops which were springing up around town. 'The Last Resort' became a skinhead mecca in the East End. 'Flip' and others in the King's Road and Covent Garden imported old US gear. Cheap imitation Crombie overcoats and tonic suits flooded the market from Asian sweatshops, cashing in on the two-tone and mod craze. Ben Sherman realised their heritage and started reproducing their button-down collar shirts. Shelley's footwear started hashing out cheap loafers and I was faced with a choice of cloning, designing and manufacturing my own gear, or looking for another career. Buying from my usual sources had become increasingly difficult, with everybody after the same things. I'd diversified as best as I could, travelling further afield for stock, but had to depend more and more on inferior copies of top-selling lines to fill my racks. What little classy top quality things I could find had to go for top dollar, beyond the budget of most of my regulars. By the late spring my heart wasn't really in it any more and by the summer it was starting to feel more like a job than an adventure into a cornucopian Narnia of fashion and style.

The thriving market hadn't escaped the notice of the taxman. A lady from the Inland Revenue did a rekkie of the market and demanded that all stall holders sign up and pay their weekly national insurance stamp. It all seemed suddenly too real. It dawned on me that the tax inspector could be our next visitor. Mildly panicking I desperately sought help from my father's accountant, the only accountant I knew or was aware of. A few calls to my dad in the states and I was all set to meet Alfred Feldman at his office in Wigmore Street. I left with him my little paper notebook where I'd meticulously inscribed every purchase and sale I'd dealt in the year or so I'd been running GAZ. I came back a fortnight later for the results. Fearing the worst I fantasised a huge tax bill and worse, being caught in an inescapable loop-the-loop, caged in the system year after year paying tax and working in a trap of my own making. Alfred, a very congenial old Jewish man, smiled and passed me back my little red book, lowered his voice and said, "burn it". Almost everything passing through my hands was strictly cash, though I had opened a bank account recently to deal with the occasional cheque. I burnt the book and let off the hook I swam for my freedom, feeling I may not be so lucky next time.

A quiet, unassuming, gay guy called Alex who occasionally frequented my shop, keen on rocksteady and always maintaining a modest skinhead style mentioned a club he was starting. He said he was modelling it on The Two-Tone Club in Oxford Street which he'd loved and hadn't seen anything like it since I'd stopped DJing there. He bought the odd record off me, traded some doubles of his rare 60's Studio Ones and gave me the address and date of his launch night.

I was with a pal, Nick Salter, in the West End on this evening. Snazzed up we hit town to see some band and felt we should investigate and show some support. Curious of what Alex's take on The Two-Tone Club would be like, we thought we'd poke our noses in.

I had heard of the place before, via a tall red-faced, know-it-all guy with no shoes and socks who often appeared at my shop, extolling the virtues of this club he was running in Soho. I was always a little wary of him as his eyes were constantly blood-shot and, suspicious that he was probably a junkie, I never gave it much thought. If anything I made a mental note not to ever bother visiting. Formerly known as 'Billy's', it had been temporarily home to The Blitz Club, a hangout of the new-romantic branch of the punk family, run by the slightly full-on Philip Salon we knew from Ken Market. He was a friend of Degville's in the basement of Ken Market, where guys like Boy George, dressed in priests outfits, mingled with freaks with really bad 80's hairdos and make up. The gay club scene had always been alive and well after dark and since that Saturday Night Fever film of '79 had rekindled and massively boosted the disco scene, nightclubs and discotheques were back on the map.

The blinged-up, white-suited flared trouser look, popular with the Lebanese in Edgware Road and the new-romantic scene were the antithesis to all we stood for in the dressing-up league. They all had somewhere to go but we needed somewhere to party. Nick and I had high hopes for Alex's night, though with him being such a mild guy we weren't really expecting too much of it. The name of the venue didn't help him much either, 'Gossips'. "Gossips?", we thought, "Who'd name a place Gossips?". Alex told me that it used to be known as The Mangrove in the 60's. The Beatles were reputed to have visited. We wondered why they'd ever changed the name. The Mangrove sounded dead cool, even though there was already a Mangrove in All Saints Road where we used to go and get our £5 draws.

Walking down the stairs to the basement on this seedy little cut-through between Dean Street and Wardour Street, I couldn't help feeling this uncanny sense of déja vu. I'd had a vivid dream about a place just like this when living in Wales, of entering a red womb-like basement nightclub with one of my best old Holland Park schoolmates Keith Gill. I couldn't remember the complexities of the dream, it was just another crazy dream, but it had lodged itself into my psyche, and on entering Gossips for the first time it felt weirdly like I was re-entering a half-forgotten room in my mind. Greeted by a tidy, youngish, black manager and a huge Jamaican bouncer called Bigga, being on the list we were ushered through to the far side where Alex was DJing. Nick headed straight for the Space Invaders machine in a little sunken cavern on the left. I liked the bamboo touches by the reception at the foot of the stairs and the subterranean cave-like effects. The one in front seated the barefoot red-eyed guy who seemed to be somehow involved. The tropical fish tanks by the cloakroom and the bar were cool and there were plenty of little African masks, shields and spear type decorations about the place. The bar was reasonably well stocked and nicely lit. Behind a few hefty square mirrored pillars there was the dance floor. Wooden, but with those 1960's style square Perspex tiles, lit from beneath with flashing coloured lights. On the corner of the floor facing me, was the tiny enclosed DJ booth. Alex opened an adjacent side door in the main seating and bar area and showed me the hilarious little back stage area and way to the DJ booth. It was minute, no more than a few yards of narrow corridor with a lit mirror at the end, all set beneath the emergency back fire exit that led to the house above. The house above on Meard Street was actually a clip joint with a bunch of transvestites, some of who looked convincingly like women. They offered sex for money, then usually kicked out their punters high and dry minus their cash.

I wondered if I'd come too early or was I too late? I looked around the club and the only two people I could see were two fat girls dancing on the dance floor. As we were leaving soon after I made mention of this to the doorman who said: "Can you do any better?" The couple of beers we'd had that evening had made me more cocky than usual. "Suppose I can?" I replied. "Anyone could, couldn't they?"

He reeled off a few phone numbers on to a scrap of paper and gave them to me saying, "Do a night here, I'll give you forty percent of the door money. Call me when you're ready."

Back at Ken Market I asked a few friends what they thought about the idea. I told Byron, Dom and Nassa that if I did it I'd want to play not just the ska and old reggae, but all the styles of music that we loved, from the latest releases back to the earlier sounds of New Orleans Jazz. I wanted somewhere to dance to the rhythm and blues of the 40's and early 50's and the black rock'n'roll that followed it, as well as a heavy dose of James Brown, mod, soul, funk, rockabilly and whatever the hell took our mood or fancy. Staring at the piece of paper with the guy's numbers on it I pondered for a couple of weeks, thinking that maybe nobody would come to a mixed bag joint like that. Nassa was insistant, "We'll all come. Do it, it'll be brilliant." So I ceased stewing, took a deep breath and called the guy up.

His Friday nights were tied up as were his Saturdays. Like most clubs they relied on their regular nine to five weekend punters who came for the typical fare. That's how they made their bread and butter to pay their bills. But they did have Mondays to Thursdays available. Alex's night had already died a death so his night was included in that too. I said I'd like to try the Thursday night, but I'd only do it on certain conditions. A lift on the no hat, no trainers Friday-Saturday dress code policy. I wanted my own door people to create the right welcome, including my choice cloakroom girl and receptionist. I wanted fifty percent of the door and left to him to think it over while he spoke to the owner Vince. He called me back saying it was a deal as long as I covered any advertising and promotion myself. They gave me a trial run of three weeks. We verbally shook on it and set a date of July 3rd, which gave me less than a month to get the word out.

I'd been copying cassette tapes of compilations I'd been making at home at Better Badges, 286, Portobello Road, run by a longhaired guy called Jolly. Every Saturday he'd pitch up outside his premises, selling his cult badges that he'd manufactured upstairs with reggae, punk and underground slogans on them. He also sold tapes of new wave and reggae that he'd burned and for a small fee anyone could go to him with an idea or artwork and he'd bang out badges or tapes for you. I scrawled out a handwritten flyer, handed it to him and said I wanted it tri-coloured, in red, yellow and green, fading into each other. I wanted to use the same coloured sheets as backing for a load of badges with the club name, which I had just decided upon. By mid-1980 most people knew me by my nickname and now I was going to start a club, I wanted people to have an idea of what to expect so I called it GAZ'S ROCKIN' BLUES.

Flyers printed, we covered Ken Market, Camden, Portobello and Kings Road. We hit all our usual haunts and record shops, phoned around friends and family. It was to be sink or swim. I was prepared for the worst but hoping for the best and organised my records into some old wooden soft drinks crates. I asked a few friends, Big John, James Lebon and Lance to help with the door and Nassa, Dom and Byron to help with the records, Fiona, who had a stall in Ken Market, to do the cloakroom and someone else to do the till. Because I knew so many people who would expect to be in for free I decided that there would be no guest list and only a nominal £2 entry fee that everyone could afford.

Clubs had to be membership only in those days to obtain a late night drinking and dancing licence. In order to be legal one had to be a member for 24 hours. I was determined to find a way around this so bought a membership book and proceeded to fill it with as many friends as possible and offered free membership on the night, back-dated by a day or so. I had membership cards printed that were to be for life, as well as gold on black business cards. I still have my membership card, I'm sure many still do, but the original membership book was confiscated by police in one of their many raids years ago. If not destroyed, it's sitting in a drawer somewhere with dozens of other little treasures, culled from their endeavours to keep a lid on London.

Johnny T, Gossips,
1980

I found a place that printed on books of matches so had a few boxes of those made up. With a big bag of badges, the matches, a couple of trays of nectarines and peaches, a little green plant and a Union Jack tea towel, grabbing the record boxes we stepped out and hailed a taxi.

Our stomachs full of butterflies, with a strong sense of anticipation and loaded with excitement we headed in a straight line towards Soho, through Bayswater Road and Oxford Street, to 69 Dean Street.

THE FIRST NIGHT

Jason at Gossips,
1980

We pulled up outside the entrance nice and early around 8pm, put the badges up on the notice board in reception for people to take and put the matchbooks and bowls of fruit on each table. The records and little plants went on the table in the DJ booth and I stapled the Union Jack on its back wall. Years later they revamped the DJ booth with a more aesthetic wooden interior but at that time it was a stark, metal-rimmed, silver, plastic, tin can, badly in need of some warmth.

We anxiously awaited nine o'clock, pensive and wondering if anyone would show up apart from the faithful few. The butterflies were still playing havoc with my stomach as the first guests arrived. In no time the queue went all the way up the stairs and out on to the street, as people began filling in and collecting their membership cards. Very soon the bar room was humming with happy faces, everyone dressed to the nines. The dance floor filled fast and the whole club rocked through the night. It was rammed and absolutely buzzing. I got to play whatever I wanted and everybody liked it.

At 3.30am, half an hour after the bar shut, nobody wanted to leave. I was summoned to the office, which may once have been a coal cellar. I had to walk behind the length of the bar to reach it to get my money. There I met Vince. Not quite as immense as Bigga, but pretty big to say the least, with a large and imposing character to match. He was Bigga's boss, the club owner, a suave Jamaican with airs of a colonial gentleman. "Gary", he said coolly, using the Cary Grant pronunciation, "this club will last for three years." I was thinking, "Three years!", I couldn't imagine what three years even looked like, I was only going to do it for three weeks. If the trial period hadn't worked out I would have been fine and now this huge, slick, black guy, in a beige suit and smart hat that looked like a cross between James Brown and Mohammed Ali, was telling me, "Gary, believe me, I know what I'm saying. I've been doing this for a long time. I want a meeting with you next week and I'll prepare up a contract."

I never did sign that contract but a few of his stipulations made some sense. Mainly, he didn't want me to DJ within a reasonable radius of Gossips as long as I played there. I was happy to build a good rapport with him and his staff and work to establish a good relationship, but chiefly I was hiring the club, it was my night, I'm my own boss and what-ever I did beyond those walls was strictly my business. I picked up a nice little fat wedge, rounded up the team and everybody steamed back to my place to party the rest of the night. When we got there, Lance unfurled a lovely surprise Jeroboam of champagne. It's still to this day the biggest bottle of champagne I've ever had and I still have the bottle to remind me. After weighing everything up I realised that I could make more money in one night than I could make in a whole week in Ken Market. The second Thursday wasn't as busy as the opening night, but the third night was every bit as packed as the first. The joint was jumping and there was no turning back.

THE BANDS ARRIVE

I gave in my notice at Ken Market and the closing down sale sign went up. Funny, but it was in those last days of the market that we finally got our first and only bit of press. The newly formed i-D magazine, shooting its second edition, did a small feature on the shop, which we gleefully paraded around at the club, further boosting our cred. It was the first time I'd been in a paper since a kid, though it wasn't long until the Evening Standard picked up on us and a young TV presenter, Danny Baker, came down to do a little piece. There was no big club scene then and hardly any mention of clubs in the press, but it wouldn't be long until the scene began to snowball.

I had no intention of putting on live acts at the beginning. There didn't seem anywhere to put them; the place wasn't designed that way. There was no PA and I hardly knew any groups anyway. Then these three rockabilly guys from New York who'd been coming every night since we opened needed a gig. They had great big quiffs, cool 50's outfits and we started hanging out. I showed them around town a bit and we jammed around my house. They were the business. They were staying on the floor of a friend's flat in a tower block with their English manager, who had a clothes shop in New York not unlike mine. He brought them over to London, convinced it was the right place and time to break them. He got them onto a short London tour, supporting Geno Washington and the Ram Jam band. They called themselves The Stray Cats. Me and Nick Salter went to see them at the Nashville, West Kensington. It was seven o'clock and the place was empty. They burst on to the stage and played as if to an audience of a million. I felt a bit sorry for them and insisted that they play down the club to a proper young and with -it crowd.

It was my seventh night. We booked a PA and set them up on the dance floor. Even though the pillars partially obscured the view, it was the only slightly elevated spot big enough to put them. I thought it would create the atmosphere of an old blues juke joint, rent party style. Wholly unadvertised other than word of mouth the night was more packed than ever. People squeezed and leaned and climbed on, in and over whatever and whoever they could to see them. They were phenomenal. Sweat dripped from the ceilings as they tore the place up. They played for an hour and a half and would have played longer if the double bass hadn't snapped in two. After that I was inundated with rockabilly bands dying to play there. It was some time before I had any more live music there, but the club remained continually packed. It was the place to be, and be seen.

A brother and sister who ran a clothes store in Camden Lock who'd had some stickers made up for me recommended hiring a cruise boat on the Thames that they had connections with. I hired The Hurlingham for our fancy dress Christmas party. In readiness for the festivities I printed up cruise tickets and menus, badges and matches for Christmas and the New Year. The cruise was fantastic, a wild night, everyone made the effort and the costumes were great. In the mid-80's I dabbled again and got together with an old Jamaican blues dance promotor, Billy Vaz, and did a few more extravagant cruises on ferry boats to France, Belgium and Amsterdam.

A new, older crowd started cottoning on to the good times we were having. An art dealer, Robert Fraser, who had a gallery in Cork Street and was linked with an infamous Rolling Stones drugs bust, soon discovered the club. He knew all the hip and with it aristos who hadn't heard sounds in night clubs like we played since they were clubbing in the 60's. With his friends Sir Mark and Lady Catherine Palmer at the fore, they introduced all their prime pals to our little hole in the wall basement dive. Many became staunch regulars. Julian Lloyd, Oliver Musker and the tall charming Denny Cordell with his silver white mop of hair, who all had music and racing interests.

Mark, a horse dealer by trade with a gypsy streak, a gold tooth and a collection of old horse drawn caravans, knew my local village, Llanddewi Brefi, in Wales via an old friend. We had plenty in common and got on famously. He'd been a ted in the 50's, one of the first mods in the 60's, and stayed in the front line of the times ever since. His hair short again, casually but well dressed, he fitted right in and was popular with all our crew. Between Mark and Robert they knew just about everybody and seemed to be friends with all the stars of music and the arts. It was probably them who first brought Mick Jagger and David Bowie down to the club. The Stray Cats' success in the charts further enhanced the club's reputation, as they still frequented the club. So many bands wanted to perform there now that I finally gave in and on the 6th of November I put on another great live band, The Meteors. With the help of their eager young manager, Nick Garrard, we printed flyers and advertised in the NME. The Meteors pioneered a manic type of rock'n'roll soon to be known as 'psychobilly'. They were completely nuts and used a lot of 50's B-movie horror gimmicks and paraphernalia to great effect. Girls stood back as the dance area became a giant moshpit. The club was a mess of hurling bodies, floor to ceiling in fake blood.

The trio wanted to perform there again, as did many others, so I decided to start another night, catering for the live music angle. So from January 1981, Gaz's Rockin' Gigz opened for the next six months on Mondays every fortnight. Some of The Bodysnatchers formed a new band featuring the bubbly young Jennie, who had a fine line in mini-skirts and a hairdo like Little Richards. They'd met her down the club and together we chose their name, The Bellestars and co-wrote the song 'Having A Good Time'. They were among the first groups to play along with the Ken Market based group The El-Trains, led by Jay Strongman who had a stall there. The Meteors and The Bellestars got records deals and started to do quite well for themselves but most of the bands at least had a West End venue to headline and invite their mates to. The psychotic Meteors' shows were rammed, completely mad and tons of fun, but many of the Mondays became a bit of a struggle to fill. By the summer I folded the Mondays and with the help of my new regular PA set-up, run by Robin Muir, I started featuring the odd band on my Thursday nights. Rob and I became great friends and still work together these days, him being responsible for our huge rig at Carnival.

One of the highlights and good things that came out of the Monday night 'Gigz' was getting hold of the 60's psycho, rock'n'roll legend Screaming Lord Sutch to play. Courtesy of Nick Garrard, who lined it all up, it was mid-May and his screaming Lordship put on an incredible show. I'd never seen so many props. There were giant axes, severed heads and people in police's uniforms chasing Sutch, who in turn chased them around the club in a pig's head mask. He lit a huge fire on the stage and there was pandemonium. How they managed to squeeze into that dressing room I'll never know. Me and Dave Sutch got on like a house on fire and got to see each other often, both living near Portobello. I nearly stood as candidate for his Monster Raving Loony Party in Kensington and Chelsea the following year. We filmed his campaign together and over the years he played several more shows for us.

For the club's first anniversary my sister Red, a dancer and choreographer, gave the first of one of her many performances with her mime trio, Sketch. I went on to help with their management before she moved to the States for a while. Throughout '81 an array of one-nighter clubs began springing up around town. The new-romantic scene was thriving and so was Gaz's. Magazines like Cosmopolitan remarked on it and by December The Sunday Times did a big feature in their colour supplement. My old friend, Ace boss Ted Carroll, who'd been down most weeks with free promos of LPs from his burgeoning catalogue, let me have a stab at compiling one for him. It was released in time for Christmas. Titled 'Gaz's Rockin' Blues', it had a great sleeve featuring cool black and white snaps taken at the club. I had copies to dish out and sell there. Every year from 1979 on I'd make up personalised Christmas cards. This year there was a picture of me and my first long-term girlfriend, Coral, with her baby daughter Colleen. We were

inseparable for over a year and she took to manning the till in reception. We had a big fancy dress party at the club on Christmas Eve and ended the year on an all time high, with an unforgettable New Year's Eve party.

My dad was in town and at fairly short notice I booked him to play live, backed by the best authentic New Orleans R&B band in town, Diz and the Doormen. Alexis Korner joined the bill as special guest and 700 people queued to get in. It was the busiest night Gossips had ever seen with a line stretching right around the block. Red and my brothers Ben and Jason were there and a whole world of friends. John and the band played an awesome set, Alexis sang a beautiful rendition of Sam Cooke's 'Bring It On Home', and together they blasted the roof off the building. It was the perfect climax to the perfect year.

Gaz 1980, taken for the Evening Standard

Left:
Big Jay Monque'D from New Orleans

30ᵗʰ DEC. 1982
GOSSIPS. 69, DEAN ST. W.1.

GAZ's
ROCKIN'
BLUES

10 - 3·30am

ADM. £2·50 (members)   £3·00 (guests)

N' BLUES

SENTS

RS EVE

LAR

COME EARLY!

DIZ & THE DOORMEN

ALEXIS KORNER

GAZ I DJ

SPECIAL GUESTS

-3·30AM. GOSSIPS, 69 DEAN ST. W.I.

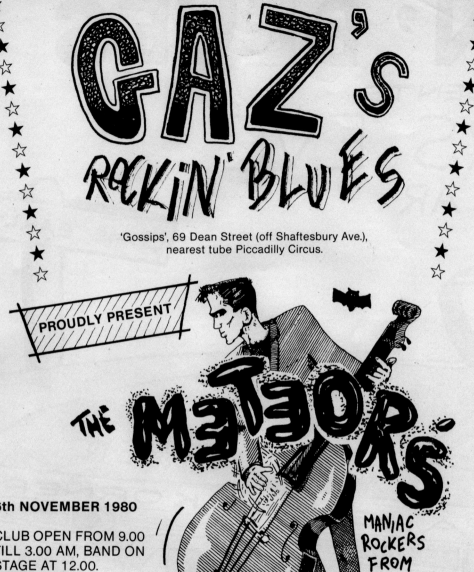

GAZ'S ROCKIN' BLUES

'Gossips', 69 Dean Street (off Shaftesbury Ave.),
nearest tube Piccadilly Circus.

PROUDLY PRESENT

THE METEORS

MANIAC ROCKERS FROM HELL!

6th NOVEMBER 1980

CLUB OPEN FROM 9.00
TILL 3.00 AM, BAND ON
STAGE AT 12.00.
SO DON'T BE LATE!!

MEMBERSHIP

The Meteors

Dingwalls

EUPHORIC from the cheap beer they're plied with before 10 o'clock, the Dingwalls Set start breaking into the fivers and drink away the long hours before the main act.

The Meteors, call themselves Psychobilly (psycho as in Hitchcock). The short, rotund lead singer/guitarist, P. Paul Fenech, has decorated his skull with an elegant *Eraserhead* cum skinhead crop. The double-bassist looks like one of those vulnerable, mid-west

psychopaths you see in films about deathrow; a victim of his sorry circumstances. He looked as though he might strangle his instrument, or random members of the audience if he played a bum note.

With titles like 'Maniac Rockers From Hell' how could they fail.

I felt attacked by my best friend; attacked by Rock 'n' Roll.

Brer Ruthven

— Page 59
New Musical Express
18th October, 1980

Gaz with the first release on his label, 1985

last
issue

JUNE 2ᴿᴰ
1983

GOSSIP'S   69 dean street w1

GAZ'
ROCKIN'
BLUES

LAST ROCKING NITE

time to move on

FROM TILL
10PM 3AM

ADM—£2.50MEMS —3.00GUEST

†GIL-CHRIST-IAN CO-OPT

Amanda and
Duke Vin, 1985

Back from the U.S.A. ....

Levi Dexter and the Rip-chords

Live On Stage!

Rock-A-Billy Shake Down!

One Night Only!

Thursday, 17th September.

with

GAZ' ROCKIN' BLUES.
Gossips Disco' 69 Dean St.

APPEARING TONIGHT

GAG
ROC
BLU

NO
26
198

THE stargazers

TONIGHT

GAZ's ROCKIN' BLUES

PROUDLY PRESENTS FROM THE USA

ON THURSDAY 16TH SEPT. '82

5 - PIECE ACCAPELLA DOO - WOP VOCAL GROUP

14 KARAT SOUL

In town for 2 weeks only Catch 'em while you can !!

GOSSIPS, 69, DEAN ST. W.1.

ADM. members £2·50 others £3

9·30 ~ 3·30 A.M.

and onstage at 12·30 . Come early, stay late, Rock your Soul !!

GAZ's ROCKIN BLUES
LAST NITE
CHECK IT OUT FOR THE LAST TIME
GOSSIPS
69 DEAN STREET
W.1.
JUNE 2ND
1983
OPEN
10pm – 3am
ADD. £3.00
members
£2.50
THURSDAY's
LONDON's
No 1
BLUES
DANCE
END OF
AN ERA
DAWNING OF A
NEW AGE
JULY 3rd
–
JUNE 2nd

AT THE ACKLAM HALL

GAZ'S
REBEL
BLUES
ROCKERS

21st BIRTHDAY PARTY,
9-2 a.m
ADM £1·50

COME EARLY

D.J.
GAZ & friends

REBEL BLUES ROCKERS

Byron's mum had adopted a street busker she'd met blowing harp and singing through a bullet mic and mini amp in Portobello Road. Not that his voice needed any amplification. He had to be the loudest person I'd ever met. Big Jay Monque'D from New Orleans, a horse and buggy tourist guide by day and blues shouter by night. Taught by blues heroes he was one of the best mouth organists I'd ever heard. She had Byron bring him down the club. We took him under our wing and were soon jamming round a piano at my mate Julian's place in Lancaster Road. Jay loved my boogie blues style and said, "That's the man I want to play piano in my band". We wrote some new songs to add to his repertoire and played our first gig at the Bull and Gate in Kentish Town. A few days later we played live outside a record shop in Portobello Road. My cloakroom girl Fiona happened to be passing by with her ghetto blaster blaring out Gene Vincent which she promptly taped our show over. Alexis Korner was in the shop throughout and the street outside was packed with all our crew and hundreds of others. It had been snowing but the weather held up while we steamed and stormed the afternoon.

As well as a mini residency in Bob's Goodtime Blues in Bramley Road I re-launched the Monday nights at Gossips to give us a regular venue to develop the band. I called it 'Gaz's Speakeasy', after the prohibition clubs in the States that the club smacked of. Big Jay moved on to front an older bunch of guys and we branched off with our own younger, punkier, blues approach. Gaz's Rebel Blues Rockers were born. In April I hired the Acklam Hall under the Westway flyover for £50 to celebrate Coral's 21st birthday. Jim Hall and Big John helped at the door and we filled the place for a classic night with JT joining the band on his new, white electric violin that I'd just bought him. The local Ladbroke Grove Skins all turned up and I had to leap off the stage at one point to stop a confrontational young Shane MacGowan from getting a hiding from them. The band was a real buzz, something I'd always wanted to do and we had a great bunch of guys in it. Poly Styrene's husband Ady "Guitar" Bell, Little Paul on harmonica and Lloyd Gordon on a T-chest bass. The song writing, band practise and gigging took more and more of my time and began taking its toll on the club. The Monday night Speakeasy sessions were going ok but they were nowhere near as popular or busy as the Thursdays. The band was a labour of love, it was early days and we weren't taken anywhere near as seriously as the club.

Our corner of Soho had long been a hive of late night drinking and partying way before I turned up. The top floor of our address at number 69 had been home to The Gargoyle Club. A bohemian jazz nighterie famous in the 20's and 30's, it was re-discovered by a new generation of youngsters in the early 80's and redefined as a home for the budding new rap and white soul scene, featuring groups like Funkapolitan. Mark Lebon started a Monday night session there, fusing music with indie films, calling it 'Views From the Reel World'. A lot of our mutual friends were involved in that scene too so our audience spent the Monday nights split between the Speakeasy downstairs and the Gargoyle up the top. After a few months there was just too much going on in the area to support two Gaz's nights in the same venue. I folded the Speakeasy to concentrate solely on the Thursday night and my band elsewhere.

Christian, Coral and Hans, fans of comic and pulp art, began helping out with some great poster artwork at this time. During that band period of '82-'83 a fantastic acapella doo-wop group from New York called '14-Carat Soul' were touring London. Their producer and manager, who ran a record shop and label in New Jersey, booked them down my club. He loved my band and we ended up backing them up a couple of times. They were phenomenal and the best thing we'd seen since The Stray Cats. It was late October 1982 when they played their second show there when I spent most of the night flat on my back in the office behind the bar. I could hardly move, grey green with sickness. I made it through the night and returned to my bed. Three days later, on Halloween, I was rushed to hospital where I nearly died of peritonitis from a burst appendix. Ten days and ten stitches later I left St Mary's Hospital and went straight to Kensal Green cemetery for one of the saddest occasions of my life. The same night I'd been operated on, Byron had been visiting Eddie's house in Stockwell whilst a riot had raged in Brixton, spilling over onto the streets around them, and tripping on a silly amount of magic mushrooms. Eddie escorted Byron and his pal, American Ben, through the rushing mob to the nearest tube station. It was the last Eddie would ever see of him.

They made it one stop to Vauxhall, then as the doors were closing, Byron hopped out telling Ben, "This is my stop". At the inquest, the driver of the train said Byron must have run all the way between the tracks as he'd reached halfway to the next station. He was sitting on the track staring eerily into space when the train hit him. Being one of the original prime figures in our social circle it was a heavy blow to everyone who knew him and put a dark cloud over the club. While I was recovering, friends and family kept it all going and on the 9th of December I was well enough to return. In January we held a special tribute night for him and raised some money towards a headstone for him. Everyone was there, including his family friend David Hockney, who hadn't been to a London nightclub for years. He mentioned that night that one of his reasons for emigrating was that London closed at eleven o'clock and he was glad to see that things were beginning to change.

By the summer of '83 the club was really beginning to suffer, I was so distracted and preoccupied with the Rebel Blues Rockers that I decided to focus entirely on the band and set a date to call it a day. On June 2nd, almost the three years that Vince had predicted, we held what I thought may be the last ever night of Gaz's Rockin' Blues.

Meteors gig at the club, 1981

GAZ'S ROCKIN BLUES

PROUDLY PRESENTS
THE RENOWNED MASTER
OF THE TENOR SAX...
PETE THOMAS & HIS **DEEP SEA JIVERS**
+ SPECIAL GUESTS

A.M.

THURS 19TH JAN '84 9·30 - 3·30

GOSSIPS, 69 DEAN ST. SOHO W.1.

ADM. £3 MEMBERS. £3·50 GUESTS, £2 BEFORE 11PM £1 MEMBERSHIP (FREE BEFORE 11)

THIS NIGHT IS DEDICATED IN LOVING MEMORY AS A TRIBUTE TO A TRULY GREAT MAN WHO INSPIRED & FIRED THE HEARTS OF THOUSANDS. A MAN OF EXCELLENT TASTE & STYLE. STRONG IN VIRTUE, LOVED & RESPECTED BY ALL WHO KNEW HIM. ALEXIS KORNER.

GAZ'S ROCKIN BLUES

PROUDLY PRESENTS - A BENEFIT FOR THE

D.B.C.
DREAD. BROADCAST. CORP.
TRANSMITTER APPEAL FUND

GOSSIPS. 69 DEAN ST W.1.

ADM. £3 MEMBERS. £3·50
GUESTS. £2 BEFORE 11 P.M. £1 MEMBERSHIP (FREE BEFORE 11)

7·30 P.M. - 3·30 A.M.

THURS 15TH MAR '84

FEATURING
REBEL
RADIO
D.J's
+

G A Z

GAZ'S ROCKIN BLUES

GOSSIPS.
69 DEAN St W.1.
ADM. £3, MEMBERS. £3·50,
GUESTS. £2 BEFORE 11 P.M. £1 MEMBERSHIP (FREE BEFORE 11)
9·30 P.M. – 3·30 A.M.

HURS 12TH APR '84

FEATURING...
THIS WEEK ONLY
BRITAINS
LEADING
WILD
ROCKABILLY
TRIO!!
+ THE
BEST IN
BLUES &
REGGAE

GAZ'S ROCKIN BLUES

..FEATURING .... **THE** ..BLUES BUSTING..
CHICAGO BEARCATS

GOSSIPS.
69 DEAN ST W.1.
ADM. £3, MEMBERS. £3.50,
GUESTS, £2 BEFORE 11 P.M. £1 MEMBERSHIP (FREE BEFORE 11)
9.30 P.M. — 3.30 A.M.

THURSDAY 24TH JAN '85

GAZ'S ROCKIN BLUES

GOSSIPS.
69 DEAN ST W.1.
ADM. £3, MEMBERS. £3.50,
GUESTS, £2 BEFORE 11 P.M. £1 MEMBERSHIP (FREE BEFORE 11)
9.30 P.M. — 3.30 A.M.

THUR 29TH NOV
FEATURING ....PETE THOMAS & HIS RED HOT TENOR
SAXAPHONE ROCKIN' THE JOINT WITH HIS BAND...

THE **DEEP SEA JIVERS**

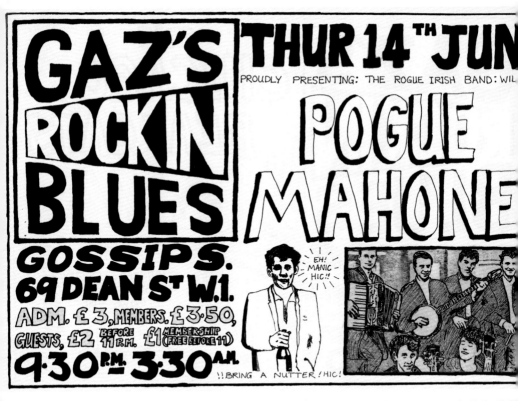

GAZ'S ROCKIN BLUES

THUR 14TH JUN

PROUDLY PRESENTING: THE ROGUE IRISH BAND: WIL

POGUE MAHONE

EH! MANIC HIC!!

GOSSIPS. 69 DEAN St W.1.

ADM. £3, MEMBERS. £3.50, GUESTS, £2 BEFORE 11 P.M. £1 MEMBERSHIP (FREE BEFORE 11)

9.30 P.M. - 3.30 A.M.

!!BRING A NUTTER! HIC!

GAZ'S ROCKIN BLUES

THUR 21ST JUN

PROUDLY PRESENTING: LONDONS WILDEST NEW COWBOY OUTFIT. ROCKABILLY OF THE OLD WEST

LASH LARIAT & THE LONG-RIDERS

GOSSIPS. 69 DEAN St W.1.

ADM. £3, MEMBERS. £3.50, GUESTS, £2 BEFORE 11 P.M. £1 MEMBERSHIP (FREE BEFORE 11)

9.30 P.M. - 3.30 A.M.

CHECK IT OUT

GAZ'S ROCKIN BLUES

GOSSIPS.
69 DEAN St W.1.

ADM. £3, MEMBERS. £3.50, GUESTS, £2 **BEFORE 11 P.M.** £1 MEMBERSHIP (FREE BEFORE 11)

9.30 P.M. - 3.30 A.M.

THURS 4th Oct

GOIN' T'GAZ'S MISTER ??

SURE, HOP IN!

PROUDLY PRESENTING

SUGAR RAY FORD & THE HOT SHOTS

GAZ'S ROCKIN BLUES

GOSSIPS.
69 DEAN St W.1.

ADM. £3, MEMBERS. £3.50, GUESTS, £2 **BEFORE 11 P.M.** £1 MEMBERSHIP (FREE BEFORE 11)

9.30 P.M. - 3.30 A.M.

PRESENTS

THE HATCHET MEN

CERT X

THURS OCT 1

GAZ'S ROCKIN BLUES
GOSSIPS. DEAN St W.1.
M. £3, MEMBERS, £3.50
TS, £2 BEFORE 11PM £1 MEMBERSHIP (FREE IF TICKET)
30 PM TO 3.30 AM

THUR 28th JUN
PROUDLY PRESENTING: THE ACE ROCKIN R&B GROUP FROM CAMDEN TOWN.....
THE HATCHET-MEN
MURDER STYLE
UN-ADULTERATED AUTHENTIC RHYTHM & BLUES!

GAZ'S ROCKIN BLUES
GOSSIPS. 69 DEAN St W.1.
ADM. £3, MEMBERS, £3.50
GUESTS, £2 BEFORE 11PM £1 MEMBERSHIP (FREE IF TICKET)
9.30 PM TO 3.30 AM

THUR 23rd AUG
PROUDLY PRESENTING.....
CAT-TALK
RED HOT ROCKABILLY, R&B SO COME & ROCK TO THE BEAT TUFF MUSIC THAT SOUNDS SWEET

GAZ'S ROCKIN BLUES
GOSSIPS. 69 DEAN St
M: £3 MEMBERS, 50 GUESTS, £2 BEFORE 11PM
30 PM TO 3.30 AM

THURS 6th SEP '84
PROUDLY PRESENTS
SUGAR RAY FORD & THE HOT SHOTS
D.J. GAZ

GAZ'S ROCKIN BLUES
GOSSIPS. 69 DEAN St W.1.
ADM. £3, MEMBERS, £3.50
GUESTS, £2 BEFORE 11PM £1 MEMBERSHIP (FREE IF TICKET)
9.30 PM TO 3.30 AM

PROUDLY PRESENTING
PETE THOMAS & THE DEEP SEA JIVERS
THUR 18th OCT

Lash Lariat & The LONGRIDERS
Matt Luke Dusty Lash
At **Gaz's Rockin Blues**
IN GOSSIPS 69 DEAN ST W1
9.30 PM - 3.30 AM
ADM. £3.50 or £2.00 BEFORE 11PM
THURSDAY 27th SEPT.

GAZ'S ROCKIN BLUES
GOSSIPS. 69 DEAN St W.1.
ADM. £3, MEMBERS, £3.50,
GUESTS, £2 BEFORE 11PM £1 MEMBERSHIP (FREE IF TICKET)
9.30 PM TO 3.30 AM

THUR 13th DEC
GREETINGS MUSIC LOVERS THIS IS YOUR HOST FROM THE CRYPT OF TERROR. WELCOME TO A NITE OF MANIC RHYTHM & BLUES FEATURING THE BAND
THE HATCHETMEN
WILD!

GAZ'S ROCKIN BLUES
GOSSIPS. 69 DEAN St W.1.
ADM. £3, MEMBERS, £3.50,
GUESTS, £2 BEFORE 11PM £1 MEMBERSHIP (FREE IF TICKET)
9.30 PM TO 3.30 AM

THUR 3rd JAN '85
STARTING OFF THE NEW YEAR WITH A TOTALLY MANIC
TOGA PARTY
PROUDLY PRESENTING LIVE FOR YOUR ENTERTAINMENT
HEY! LAY OFF BUDDY! WHAT'S HAPPENING?? WE'RE GOING TO THE TOGA PARTY THAT'S WHAT HA!
ROCHEE AND THE SARNOS

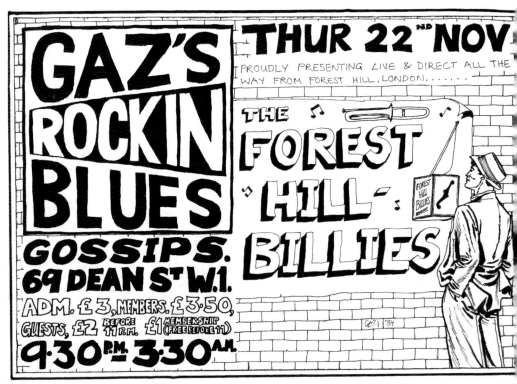

THE RE-LAUNCH

'Gaz's Rebel Blues Rockers' didn't last long. We made a 7" single, co-produced by Chas Jenkel of Ian Dury and The Blockheads fame. It was pressed in time for the Notting Hill Carnival where we played outside RISK, the clothes shop, which we rehearsed in the basement of. It proved to be our last gig. A clash of egos led to us splitting up, or should I say, I left the band. They went it alone, eventually disbanding a few months later.

For the first time in years I holidayed, read books and lounged around with my new girlfriend Little Jo. During this time I started a series of compilations 'Gaz's Rockin' Tapes', compiled from my record collection. With the help of my friend, the artist Gary Chapman, we designed great looking colourful jackets, which I eventually sold from the cloakroom of the club where they were displayed each week. While re-evaluating my life, my finances (or the lack of them) ultimately forced my hand to make a decision. I decided that I wouldn't form a new band just yet, I would bide my time until I met the right people and then make a proper go of it. Aside from that, there was only one way to make a living that I loved, could excel at and that really suited me. That was the club.

I called Mick Collins who'd managed Gossips for the past two years or so and arranged a meeting with him and Vince at a Sicilian restaurant in Dean Street. I'd had a good think and worked out exactly what was necessary to make a success of it. They agreed that I should promote more live bands and were prepared to share half the cost. Robin's PA was booked each week very reasonably and Vince chipped in for the printing of a wad of posters, which Nick Salter and I slapped up around town. We bumped the admission price a bit and got a friend, Charlie Paul, to design a great logo for the club. Hans designed a flyer for the re-launch and we opened to a packed night at the beginning of December. Eddie agreed to help with the DJing. I still did the lion's share initially but it did make a big difference having someone cover my back, making sure that discs went back into the right sleeves and boxes and keeping the music flowing if I had to run to the door, bar or loo. I loved to dance and Eddie knew just what tunes and sequence to select to get me going crazy. For the next six months we featured very few groups but by October I was booking them one a week.

Skiffle and country elements were making inroads amongst the 50's retro bands that I put on in '84. Busking friends from some of these bands, ex-Blues Rockers, The Spartans, Lash Lariat and Pogue Mahone performed to name a few, the latter having to change their name to 'The Pogues' as their original name meant 'kiss my ass' in Gaelic and was considered too offensive by the BBC. Cat, the only girl in their band came every Thursday to wreak havoc at the bar. Tom Conran, son of Habitat mogul Sir Terence, fresh out of college, came in and took over the little kitchen at the back and revolutionised the bar and food snacks. The latter he topped with little cocktail stick flags flaunting the club logo.

SKA SKA SKA

On July the 7th 1984 I was due to be at Nick and Ari Ashley's wedding in the country. I'd known Nick from Holland Park school days and couldn't opt out. The same day the legend Prince Buster was performing live with The Skatalites at the UK's first reggae Sunsplash festival in Crystal Palace. Me, Eddie and our whole posse were desperate to go. Recently reformed, it was the first time The Skatalites had ever played in the UK and the first time that Buster had been here since 1967. Obviously we'd all been huge fans since we could remember and I was gutted that I couldn't go. Then as if by magic, fate intervened and something happened that was to have a major impact on myself and the club. I got a call from another old Holland Parker, Spencer Style. His girlfriend, Isabel, worked for the magazine Black Music International. They were covering Sunsplash, short-staffed and needed someone to interview Prince Buster, and guess what?

He was staying with the band two blocks away from my house at a self-catering flat in the aptly named Prince's Square. I pocketed my pen and notepad, dashed down and knocked on the door. As it opened a cloud of smoke emanated from within. PB was out shopping and I was led through this marijuana pea-souper to wait for him in the kitchen. The place was dark as the band were all resting, the only light being the room I was in. Prince arrived and we clicked right away. He introduced me to all his friends, took photos, I nailed the interview, then went up to my place for a cup of tea. It was the beginning of a lifelong friendship.

When I returned after the wedding we started hanging out a lot. Showing him around town, I took him to a champagne reception of an art exhibition at the Royal Academy in Piccadilly, where to everyone's delight he met some of the gang. On Thursday he came to the club and met the rest. Prior to this most of us imagined him as some kind of mythical creature and here he was, hanging out with us. He loved our scene and said that it made him feel like he was sixteen all over again. When The Skatalites went back to Jamaica, Prince changed his ticket and checked into a hotel a few yards up the road from me and we hung out for the next three months. I helped him do a little detective work, retracing what had happened to his back catalogue stock since the death of Melodisc entrepreneur Emile Shallet, his mentor and UK label boss. We located and pulled it all together under one roof, which he rewarded me for with hundreds of rare old Blue Beat and Fab singles. I called Joe Strummer, who lived locally, asking him if he'd like to meet Prince Buster. He was gobsmacked and that evening he came to dinner with his missus Gaby Salter and their new baby. Joe later got his revenge asking me if I'd like to meet Robert De Niro, who he summarily brought down to the club.

We finished the year, partly through Buster's influence, by managing to get Desmond Dekker to play our Christmas party. He was amazing and just as good as he'd ever been. Joe came along; it was a wild and sweaty night, opening the door to a new era of ska and reggae legends that were to appear at the club for us in the coming years. In March I launched my last short-lived attempt at a Monday night venture. This time in Stockwell, near Rock Steady Eddie's place. Here I met Trevor, the drummer of a new instrumental ska band called 'The Potato 5'. I had a budget of £25 a week for bands. They wanted to play but I told them to come back when they had a singer, which they duly did, from Jamaica, Floyd Loyd Seivright who'd come through Alpha Boys School. I gave them a slot at my big 5th anniversary extravaganza when one of the bands (The Elevators) pulled out. This show was possibly a little too ambitious. I'd hired the Univeristy of London Union hall in Bloomsbury. Joe Strummer lent us a couple of grand and Spencer Style and I put on a fabulous night with seventeen bands set in three big rooms. It was a great achievement but we lost a lot of money. It took a year for us to pay Joe back. It was the first time I'd got pioneer soundman Duke Vin to play for us. Prince had said to me that I couldn't know music until I knew Mr "Shiny Shoes" Vinny.

Vin was the first DJ in Jamaica. He'd stowed away on a banana boat with Count Suckle in 1953 and started the very first sound-system in England in '55, living in West London ever since. He used to play at The Flamingo Club in Wardour Street and hadn't seen Georgie Fame since that time. It was wonderful to get them together on the same bill.

I'd been to the Flamingo. Run by the Gunnell brothers who managed my dad and Georgie Fame, it was the most influential R&B club in town in its day and had been to London what the Cavern had been to Liverpool. After it closed the Marquee took over its mantel, being another place I'd visited as a child. These two clubs were almost templates for my Rockin' Blues. Alexis Korner had run Monday and Thursday sessions at them both and I was so glad that he got to be part of what I was doing, revitalising the club blues scene in Soho, before he passed away in '84. At the ULU event I was particularly impressed by The Potato 5, finding it hard to believe they couldn't even get a gig in town for a meagre £25. I promised to help them and became their manager for the following year. I booked them a monthly slot at my night at Gossips and went to Dave Robinson, the boss of Stiff Records, to get them a deal.

My old friend Damian Korner engineered the sessions and my brother Jason, now back from the States, helped negotiate and designed the label art. 'Gaz's Rockin' Records' was born with The Potato 5's debut single, 'Western Special'. It was soon followed by their first 12". They were picked up by the mainstream music press to great appraisal. I got them an agent and some big shows around town. With their ascendancy and regular appearances at the club they introduced a lot of new ska fans into the mix. Spence introduced me to one of the original pioneers, the man I tagged the 'Godfather of ska', Laurel Aitken. It was at a studio in Brixton where he was spending his last few bob recording a disco 12", I said I had the perfect band for him and a ready-made audience of fans who would adore him. He did a couple of shows at the club. I linked him up with The Potato 5, who loved him, and soon we were in the studio recording four tunes of his that I'd selected. Stiff records split from Island records after some fallout with Chris Blackwell so I couldn't put out my next two singles of Laurel's. I raised the money and released them wholly independently, receiving the top singles of the week review in NME in '86.

I DJ'd for my first time in Japan around that time and convinced my promotor and friend Masa Hidaka to bring Laurel and "The Spuds" over as soon as possible. Together with his friend, the journalist, Koichi Hanafusa, who'd first introduced us, they linked up a nice licensing deal and tour for the following year, kick-starting a huge ska scene over there. That summer Lee Perry was in town and I flukily booked him for a one-off show. I'd been a fan since teaching myself to play drums to his 'Return Of Django' years before when I was a teenage skinhead. He was a front-line innovator and mad as a hatter. It was a real coup. He arrived early for sound-check and spent the first two hours back stage studying the graffiti on the walls with a torch. He then added his own statements like "I kill the devil dead". He then built himself an obeah altar by the mirror at the back, hanging up broken pieces of scissors and other strange objects from the strip bulb. He came on stage dressed head to toe in Union Jacks, with the torch around his neck and a big spliff in his mouth, much to the horror of Bigga the bouncer who seemed powerless to intervene.

At the end of '86 I formed a new band, 'The Trojans'. By the time I went to Japan in mid '87 with Laurel, The Trojans had already recorded a couple of singles for my label and we'd played our first few shows at the club and elsewhere. Laurel and The Potato 5 went down a storm in Japan. The Japs adored my new single 'Ringo', which I'd sung entirely in Japanese. On the bill was a great new Japanese ska band called 'The Ska Flames'. I promised to record them if they could get to London, which in 1988 they did. I got them onto a stage at Notting Hill Carnival and managed to record a whole album in a day, which I eventually released here and in Japan.

Gaz, 1987
Spirit of Adventure

The Flames' gig at the club blew people's minds. Their original line-up, energy and style were second to none and I'm glad to see they're still going strong today.

In '88, my lot, The Trojans, toured Japan promoting the first of many albums released over there, thus forging and solidifying my east-west links and a lifelong love affair with Japan.

Over the ensuing years I was lucky to feature some of the greatest names in the history of ska. Derrick Morgan, Justin Hinds, Delrow Wilson, Alton Ellis and London's own Bad Manners. Prince Buster even got up and sang some skat one night with The Potato 5. We recorded a hot version of 'Stack-A-Lee' together which we played with The Trojans at a memorable ska festival in Finsbury Park. From 1989 and for nearly ten years, Gaz's Rockin' Blues was the hub of the UK ska scene. If you wanted to hear the real deal, it was the top spot in town and you had to come down.

GAZ'S ROCKIN BLUES

GOSSIPS.
69 DEAN ST. W.1.

ADM. £3.50, MEMBERS. £4,
GUESTS. £2.50 BEFORE 11. £1 MEMBERSHIP (FREE BEFORE 11).

9.30 P.M. 3.30 A.M.

ESMOND
THUR
20TH
DEC '84
HEAVYWEIGHT R&B/SKA!
ROCK STEADY SESSION
XMAS PARTY SPECIAL
PRIZES
RAFFLE
SHUFFLING
COMPETITION
DEKKER

GAZ'S ROCKIN BLUES

GOSSIPS.
69 DEAN ST W.1.
ADM. £3, MEMBERS. £3.50,
GUESTS, £2 BEFORE 11 P.M. £1 MEMBERSHIP (FREE BEFORE 11)
9.30 P.M. - 3.30 A.M.

31ST JAN
AGNIFICENT
SEVEN
D.! COME
AZ'S FOR A
WESTERN
WILD!!
LD
AYER

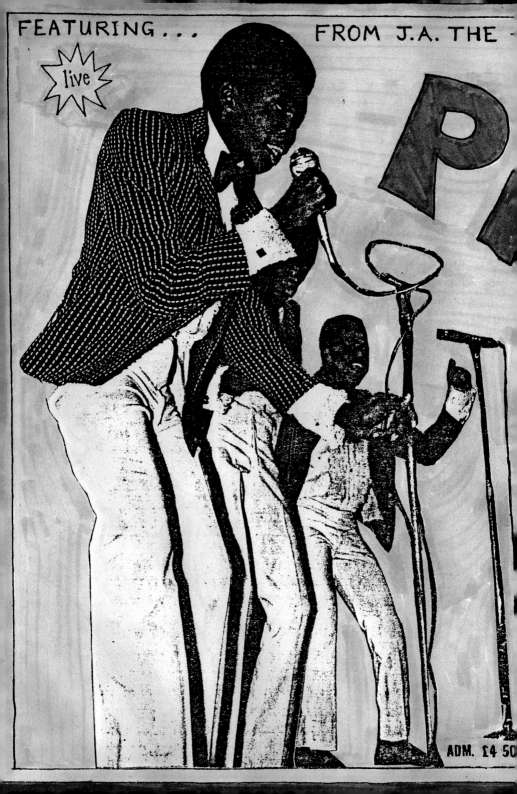

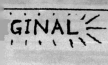
GINAL

THUR 20TH JUN '85

GAZ'S ROCKIN BLUES

AT GOSSIPS
69 DEAN ST. W1

9.30 P.M. - 3.30 A.M.

ONEERS

IFIE MAN

OOR RAMESES

ONG SHOT (KICK DE BUCKET)

OCK STEADY PARTY SPECIAL...

£3.50 MEMBERS   £2.50 BEFORE 11 P.M.   MEMBERSHIP £1   (FREE BEFORE 11)

GAZ'S ROCKIN BLUES

THUR 14th FEB

VALENTINES DAY

FANCY DRESS PARTY

PROUDLY PRESENTING..

THE KEYTONES

GOSSIPS.
69 DEAN St W.1.

ADM. £3, MEMBERS. £3.50,

GUESTS. £2 BEFORE 11 P.M. £1 MEMBERSHIP (FREE BEFORE 11)

9.30 P.M - 3.30 A.M.

GAZ'S ROCKIN BLUES

LASH LARIAT AND THE LONG RIDERS

GOSSIPS.
69 DEAN St W.1.

ADM. £3, MEMBERS £3.50

GUESTS, £2 BEFORE 11 P.M. £1 MEMBERSHIP (FREE BEFORE 11)

9.30 P.M - 3.30 A.M.

THUR 7TH FEB

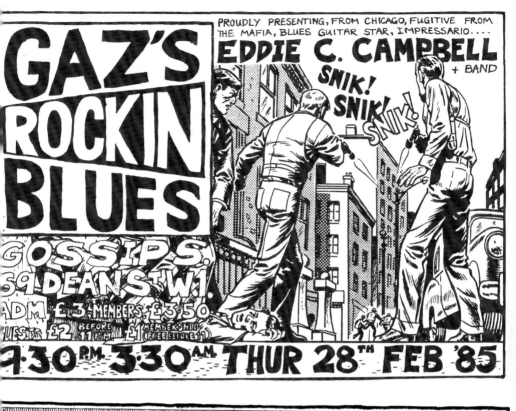

GAZ'S ROCKIN BLUES

THUR 11TH APRIL '85

PROUDLY PRESENTING LIVE..

Alton Ellis

HEAVYWEIGHT SESSION
R&B/SKA

ROCK STEADY PARTY

FEATURING THE LEGENDARY
JAMAICAN SOUL SINGER.

ALTON ELLIS

GOSSIPS.
69 DEAN St W.1.
ADM. £3.50, MEMBERS. £4,
GUESTS. £2.50 BEFORE 11. £1 MEMBERSHIP (FREE BEFORE 11).
9.30 PM - 3.30 AM.

GAZ'S ROCKIN BLUES

THE HATCHETMEN
GOOD ROCKIN BLUES

GOSSIPS.
69 DEAN ST W.1
ADM. £3, MEMBERS. £3.50
GUESTS. £2 BEFORE 11 P.M. £1 MEMBERSHIP (FREE BEFORE 11)
9.30 P.M. - 3.30 A.M.

THURSDAY 28TH MAR

littlewillie littlefeld

THURS 18TH APRIL

AT GOSSIPS
69 DEAN ST. W1

live

ADM. £3.50 MEMBERS   £4 GUESTS
£2.50 BEFORE 11 P.M.
MEMBERSHIP £1
(FREE BEFORE 11)

GAZ'S ROCKIN BLUES

+ THE HATCHETMEN

ROCKIN' THE BLUES

During the mid 80's, I'd made some good contacts with blues promotors that enabled me to book some of the big names in the R&B field. Nappy Brown was outstanding. He ended the night humping the stage with his mic-stand, pleading, "*night time is the right time to be with the one you love*". Ray Charles made it famous but Nappy Brown wrote it. He had a powerful voice inspired by his gospel roots and the night was filmed, though unfortunately he never gave written consent to release the footage. Frankie Ford, whose 'Sea Cruise' was a staple tune in the club's diet, put on a great show. Me with my brother Ben on bass backed Louisiana Red, another of the greats. Little Willie Littlefield who wrote 'Kansas City' rocked the house on a few occasions; whilst the man with the 3-D sound, Big Jay McNeely, with his fluorescent tenor saxophone, was astounding.

Original 50's rockabilly heroes, Ray Campi, Mac Curtis, Ronnie Dawson and Sleepy LaBeef graced us with great live sets. All the while, these shows were promoted each week with great poster artwork courtesy of Andrew Crawford. We'd been to Holland Park together and remained close thereafter. He played bass in The Trojans. He'd been to art college and studied graphics and was a far superior finisher than I. I'd tell him roughly what I'd want, which he would execute perfectly. He was also responsible for a lot of my record label artwork. In 1992 fearing a second bout of deep depression and the breakdown of his current relationship, he committed suicide. This knocked the stuffing out of The Trojans and all our friends sideways. No one saw it coming, only after he died was it that I noticed some of his club flyers had been showing some strange hints of what was to come. 'The Maroon Town' poster of May '91 and the 'Big Joe Louis' one in August certainly showed ominous tendencies. It was a sad time but the show had to go on.

My brother Ben joined the band after Rick Baxendale had taken over from Andrew for a year. The band coped, but the artwork suffered badly, as I was forced to recycle Andrew's artwork where possible and try and improve my own attempts. In September '93 things took another turn for the worse. Gossips' management stopped paying half the band fees, leaving me to fork out for the whole lot. It was more than I could afford out of the door money, after all my other overheads. Bands that had received whatever they were used to weren't going to suddenly drop their fee by half, so musically standards dropped. I compensated by drastically reducing the amount of live bands. I entered '94 with virtually no bands whatsoever, until the spring when a collaboration with Ian Dury introduced an act featuring a wheelchair bound robot called Ruby Throat. I always thought their song 'Easy Squeezy' should have been a number one hit. Ian loved the club. He came back to be filmed there for a TV programme about his favourite places in London and sadly died not so long after it was aired. To cap it all, Gossips was plagued with renovations. Each week another part of the club was boarded off. It was like trying to run a club in a building site. We'd been forced to move the DJ decks and dance floor to the other side of the club a while back. This was mainly due to a dreadful guy, a lawyer, who'd bought a flat upstairs during the gentrification of Meard Street. He constantly complained about the noise below. It totally changed the club's dynamics.

On the plus side, Count Cassavubu was now with us having just left uni. Eddie was consistently rocksteady, still collecting me from home, DJing all night and then dropping me home after, so I could have the odd drink. We still had a few great acts who were happy just to come and play, regardless of the money, but by and large you could feel and see the decline. Gradually the numbers of punters dipped too. The last straw was in November, they had to close the entire club for one week when they renovated the loos and had all the plumbing out. Vince told Mick to tell me that when I came back after the loos were fixed, he wanted absolutely no bands any more. He was adamant. I asked why and was told, "They abuse the guest-list and scribble on the walls".

Overleaf:
Gaz and Rock
Steady Eddie
on Gaz's Rockin'
Cruise, October
19th, 1985

The whole of Dean Street was going upmarket and he wanted to fit in accordingly. My mind harkened back to some of the legendary stars, including Lee Perry, who'd tagged the back stage corridor. I told them, "The guest-list will always be abused and by the way can I have that back wall, please? I'll take it home and frame it." That following Thursday when we closed, Mick had kindly set up a fill-in night around the corner at a friend of his' club, St Moritz, and stood on Gossips's doorstep directing people there. I hadn't cancelled any bands that were lined up as yet and I thought I'd have a look at this new place and weigh it up.

I tried it out that week. I met the owner Sweetie and the manager Roger, I liked it, I liked it a lot, and so did everyone else. I never looked back.

THURS 16TH MAY '85

FEATURING THE MANIC ROCKABILLY BAND FROM PORTSMOUTH THE...

CARAVANS ♪

ADM. £3. MEMBERS   £3.50 GUESTS

£2 BEFORE 11 P.M.   9.30 P.M.-3.30 A.M.

live

* MEMBERSHIP £1   (FREE BEFORE 11)

GOSSIPS.
69 DEAN ST W.1.

GAZ'S ROCKIN BLUES

GAZ'S ROCKIN BLUES

GOOD ROCKIN BLOCK
& THE
ROADMASTERS

HEY! LISTEN FOLKS, COME ALONG TO THE ROCKINEST BLUES DANCE IN TOWN & SEE THIS WILD NEW R&B BAND TEARIN' UP THE AREA WITH SOME CRAZY MUSIC

THURSDAY
2nd
MAY '85

GOSSIPS.
69 DEAN St W.1.
ADM. £3, MEMBERS. £3.50, GUESTS, £2 BEFORE 11PM. £1 MEMBERSHIP (FREE BEFORE 11)
9.30 PM – 3.30 AM

THURSDAY 9TH MAY '85.

PROUDLY PRESENTING

GAZ'S
ROCKIN
BLUES

THE FEATURING WILDC
P A U L A N S E L L

BLUE
RHYTHM
BOYS

GOSSIPS
69 DEAN St W.

live

9.30PM-3.30A.M.

ADM. £3 MEMBERS £3.50 GUESTS £2 BEFORE 11PM MEMBERSHIP £1 (FREE BEFORE

GAZ'S ROCKIN BLUES

THE MAD BAD MISSOURI BUFFALOES

GOSSIPS.
69 DEAN St. W.1.

ADM. £3, MEMBERS. £4

GUESTS. £3 BEFORE 11 P.M. £1 MEMBERSHIP (FREE BEFORE 11)

9·30 P.M. - 3·30 A.M.

APPEARING THURSDAY 1st AUGUST.

LIVE!

GAZ'S ROCKIN BLUES

PROUDLY PRESENTING THE......

JUMPIN' JEHOSOPHATS

THUR 6th JUNE '85

GOSSIPS.
69 DEAN St W.1.

ADM. £3, MEMBERS. £4.

GUESTS. £2 11 P.M. £1 MEMBERSHIP (FREE BEFORE 11 P.M)

9·30 P.M. 3·30 A.M.

GAZ'S ROCKIN BLUES

THURS 4th APRIL '8

PROUDLY PRESENTS

RICKY COOL & THE BIG TOWN PLAYBOYS

GOSSIPS.
69 DEAN St

ADM. £3 MEMBERS. £3·50 GUESTS. £2 BEFORE 11 P.M.

9·30 P.M. 3·30 A.M.

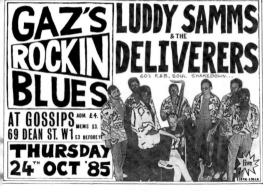

GAZ'S ROCKIN BLUES

LUDDY SAMMS & THE DELIVERERS

60's R&B, SOUL SHAKEDOWN...

AT GOSSIPS
69 DEAN ST. W1

ADM. £4
MEMS. £3.
£3 BEFORE 11

THURSDAY 24th OCT '85

LIVE

GAZ'S ROCKIN BLUES

THUR 19th SEPT

PROUDLEY PRESENTS

SKA EXPLOSION

THE POTATO

featuring Singer Floyd Ll...

LIVE

GOSSIPS
69 DEAN St. W.1.

ADM. £3, MEMBERS. £4

GUESTS. £3 BEFORE 11 P.M. £1 MEMBERSHIP (FREE BEFORE 11)

9·30 P.M. 3·30 A.M.

GAZ'S ROCKIN BLUES

ossips', 69 Dean Street (off Shaftesbury Ave.)

THU 25TH JUL '85

PROUDLY PRESENTING.. LEADER OF THE "MONSTER RAVING LOONEY PARTY" LIVE!

SCREAMING
LORD SUTCH
& THE SAVAGES

9.30 P.M.-3.30 A.M.

ADM. £3.50 MEMBERS £4 GUESTS

£3. BEFORE 11 P.M.

MEMBERSHIP £1

GAZ'S ROCKIN BLUES

Proudley Presents

THUR 18th JULY '85

♦SKA EXPLOSION♦

THE **POTATO** Five

featuring Singer Floyd Lloyd

live

GOSSIPS
69 DEAN St W.1.
ADM. £3, MEMBERS. £4
GUESTS. £3 BEFORE 11 P.M. £1 MEMBERSHIP (FREE BEFORE 11)
9·30 P.M. - 3·30 A.M.

GAZ'S ROCKIN BLUES

FEATURING ACCAPELLA ♪ FROM THE.... **MINT JULEPS**

THURSDAY 3RD OCT '85

AT GOSSIPS 69 DEAN ST. W1

ADM. £4.
MEMS £3.50
£3 BEFORE 11 P.M.

9.30 P.M. - 3.30 A.M.

Laurel Aitken in
Meard Street, 1987.
Photo by Phoenix
J Bay

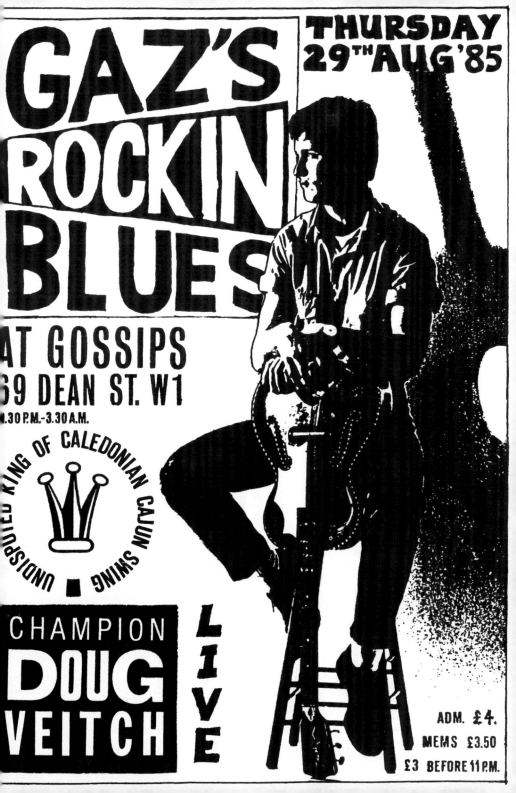

WHEN ARTIST TRACEY EMIN USED TO BE CLOAKROOM GIRL, BACK IN THE VERY EARLY DAYS OF THE CLUB, ON RECOMMENDING THE JOB TO HER...

"GARY SAID, 'IT'S A VERY SOCIAL JOB, BUT WITH VERY UNSOCIAL HOURS.'

"...ONE OF THE BEST JOBS I EVER HAD FOR MOANS." TRACEY EMIN

ONE NIGHT WHEN TRACEY ARRIVED LATE FOR WORK
THE BOUNCER BIGGA SAID:

"YOU'RE LATE." TO WHICH SHE RETORTED, "YOU'RE LUCKY, BIGGA."

SHE WAS RIGHT, WE WERE LUCKY TO HAVE HER,
AS WE HAVE BEEN WITH ALL THE GREAT GIRLS WE'VE
BEEN BLESSED TO HAVE REPRESENTING US
DOWN THERE OVER THE YEARS.

THE INSTIGATORS

FEATURING ... COURTNEY (LEAD VOCALS) + FULL HORN SECTION FOR A WILD
& CRAZY NIGHT OF ROOTS BLUES, SKA, ROCK STEADY REGGAE, IT AGO WICKED

ADM. £4. MEMBERS £4.50 GUESTS £3. BEFORE 11PM. MEMBERSHIP £1 (FREE BEFORE 11)

THURSDAY 7TH NOV '85

live & Rockin'

GOSSIPS. 69 DEAN ST W.1.

GAZ'S ROCKIN BLUES

9.30 P.M.-3.30 A.

PROUDLY PRESENTING FROM THE U.K. ADM. £3. MEMBERS £4. GUESTS £3. BEFORE 11PM. MEMBERSHIP £1 (FREE BEFORE 11)

THURSDAY 10TH OCT 1985

THE JUMPING JEHOSOPHATS

GAZ'S ROCKIN BLUES

BLUES FANS NOTICE !!
R.L. BURNSIDE HAD TO CANCEL HIS TOUR OF EUROPE & LONDON Including HIS SCHEDULED DATE AT GAZ'S

9.30 P.M.-3.30 A.M.

GOSSIPS. 69 DEAN ST W.1.

GAZ'S ROCKIN BLUES

LAUREL AITKEN

live
9.30 P.M.–3.30 A.M.

Laurel Aitken

Laurel Aitken the hit maker

SKA & BLUE BEAT, BLUES MOVEMENT

ORIGINAL BLUE BEAT & SKA MAN & HIS BAND

The musical career of Laurel Aitken stretches back to the late 50s when the Jamaican music scene was beginning to take off. *Nightfall, Boogie, In My Soul, More Whisky, Little Sheila* and *Judgement* are all examples of Laurel's 1950 hits.

In England, where ska was known as blue beat, a young girl called Millie Small stormed the British chart with the monster hit *My Boy Lollipop* in 1964. This hit opened the floodgates for Jamaican music in England, which up to then was an underground music form played in shebeens and basements of Westindian immigrants' houses, mostly on weekends.

Laurel Aitken, along with fellow singers Jackie Edwards, Owen Grey, Desmond Dekker and Derrick Morgan, hit the shores of England to promote ska's infectious rhythm.

The major labels catering for ethnic music based in England at that time, Blue Beat run by Emil Shalit Music and Island Records run by Chris Blackwell (himself a Jamaican immigrant). On these labels, Laurel pushed out hits such as *In My Soul, One More River To Cross, I Shall Remove* and *Boat To Move.*

Labels run by Rita King in Stamford Hill, Tottenham, London, called R&B Discs and Ska Beat put some of Laurel's hits such as *Propaganda, Zion, Jamboree, Lookin' For My Baby, Green Banana, Darling, You Was Up, Let My People Go* and *Bachelor Life.*

Another small label, Rio, churned out more of Laurel's hits: *Mary, Home Town, Fire, Freedom, Peace Perfect Peace, Rock Of Ages, The Saints Leave Me Standing, Bug-A-Boo, John Saw Them Coming, Jericho, Mary Don't Weep, Mary We Shall Overcome* and *Let's Be Lovers.*

Around 1968 Laurel went to Pama Records and released such hits as *Landlords and Tenants, Everybody Suffering, Woppi King, Give Me Back My Dignity, Pussy Price Gone Up, Pussy Hab Nine Life, Deal In Brixton Market, Blues Dance, Nobody But Mr Popcorn, Suffering Still* and *Sho-Be-Do (Everythin's All Right Uptight).*

Around 1979 Laurel again hit the limelight, along with his musical rival Prince Buster, when ska hit the top charts with white groups such as Madness, The Specials, Bad Manners and Selector.

By Lionel Young.

CRC-297
Vocal with Orchestra
TRIBUTE TO COLLIE SMITH
(Abrahams-Aitken)
LAUREL AITKEN and the Boogie Cats
CARIBBEAN RECORDING CO LTD
CARIBOU
MADE IN JAMAICA

DOWN BEAT
45 RPM HIGH FIDELITY
CARIBBEAN RECORDING CO. LTD.
Time 2:13
CRC 290
I'M CRYING OVER YOU
(R Abrahams - L Aitken)
LAUREL AITKEN and the Boogie Cats
MADE IN JAMAICA

Duke Reid's
Low Down Dirty Girl
(LAUREL AITKEN)
LAUREL AITKEN
MANUFACTURED BY FEDERAL RECORDS MFG CO

CR-60-602
2.23
COSW-0068
45 RPM
WHOLE LOT OF ROCK
(Abrahams-Aitken)
LAUREL AITKEN and, The Boogie Cats

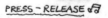
PRESS - RELEASE

AT

GOSSIPS. 69 DEAN ST W.1.

LAUREL

9.30 P.M.-3.30 A.M.

ADM. £4.

SKA

R&B

EL CUBANA

ROCK STEADY

LIVE & ROCKIN

AITKEN

£4 50 GUESTS   £3. BEFORE 11 P.M.   MEMBERSHIP £1   (FREE BEFORE 11)

"LEGEND" ORIGINAL BLUE BEAT & SKA MAN + BAND ♪

AT GOSSIPS
69 DEAN ST. W1

WEST-INDIAN
FOOD
AT THE BAR

ON THURSDAY 21ST NOVEMBER 1985

GAZ'S
ROCKIN
BLUES

GAZ'S ROCKIN BLUES

RIVERSIDE TRIO

9.30 P.M.-3.30 A.M.

Country
Hillbilly
Blues

live

THURSDAY 31ST OCT '85

AT GOSSIPS
69 DEAN ST. W1

ADM. £4.
MEMS £3.
£3 BEFORE 11 P.M.

GAZ'S ROCKIN BLUES

PRESENTS...

RED HOT N BLUE

live

(L.P. OUT NOW, ON NORTHWOOD RECORDS)

PLUS! FROM ST. ALBANS

THE DELTAS

ROCKABILLY DOUBLE FEATURE SPECIAL!

RAW WILD

GOSSIPS. 69 DEAN ST W.I.

ADM. £3.50 MEMBERS | £4 GUESTS | £3. BEFORE 11 P.M.

MEMBERSHIP £1 (FREE BEFORE 11) 9.30 P.M.-3.30 A.M.

L-R
Dave Bourne — Drums
Ashley Kingman — Guitar
Andy Bourne — Bass
Mousie — Vocals

THURSDAY 5TH DEC '85

GAZ'S ROCKIN BLUES

AT GOSSIPS.
69 DEAN ST W.1.

ADM. £4.   MEMS £3.   £3 BEFORE 11 P.M.

SKA & BLUE BEAT,
BLUES MOVEMENT

featuring...
Hot New All-Girl
Bluesbeat Band!

ON.   8.30 P.M.-3.30 A.M.

THURSDAY 19TH DEC '85

PROUDLY PRESENTING

THE

DELTONES

Rock Steady Eddie
and Gaz, 1986
Bouncing Spring
Ball in Camden
Electric Ballroom

GAZ'S ROCKIN BLUES

ADM. £4.50   MEMS £3.50   £3 BEFORE 11 P.M.

Louisiana RED

LEGENDARY US BLUES STAR

9.30 P.M. - 3.30 A.M.

PLUS

— BLOCK —

GOOD ROCKIN BLOCK & BAND

— LOUISIANA RED —

GAZ'S ROCKIN BLUES

RICKY COOL & THE BIG TOWN PLAYBOYS

THURSDAY JAN 16 – 86

GOSSIPS
DEAN ST. W1

ADM. £4.
MEMS £3.50
£3 BEFORE 11 P.M.

9.30 P.M.–3.30 A.M.

GAZ'S ROCKIN BLUES

GOSSIPS.
69 DEAN St W.1.

THURSDAY
30TH JAN '86

PRESENTS...
THE jumPing Jehosophats!

ADM. £4.
MEMS £3.50
£3 BEFORE 11 P.M.

9.30 P.M.–3.30 A.M.

GAZ'S ROCKIN BLUES

APPEARING LIVE ON —

THURSDAY
— 20th FEB '86 —

Rhythm and Blues WITH

- GEORGIE ·
— FAME —
& THE ☆
BLUE FLAMES

AT GOSSIPS
69 DEAN ST. W1

ADM. £5

MEMS £4.

— £3 BEFORE 11 P.M. —

· MEMBERSHIP £1 · FREE BEFORE 11 PM ·

9.30 P.M. - 3.30 A.M.

PROUDLY PRESENTS

GAZ'S ROCKIN BLUES

AT GOSSIPS
9 DEAN ST. W1
9.30 P.M.-3.30 A.M.

LUDDY SAMMS
— AND THE —
DELIVERERS

THURS 23 JANUARY · 1986

ADM. £4. MEMS £3.50 £3 BEFORE 11 P.M.

GAZ'S ROCKIN BLUES

GOSSIPS.
9 DEAN ST W.1.

£4. MEMS £3. £3 BEFORE 11 P.M.

SKA & BLUE BEAT,
BLUES MOVEMENT

Featuring...
Hot New All-Girl
Bluesbeat Band!

8.30 P.M.-3.30 A.M.

THURSDAY,
4th A APRIL '86·

PROUDLY PRESENTING
THE
DELTONES

GREAT

WILD♪

PRESENTS...

GAZ'S ROCKIN BLUES

THE jumping

ADM. £4.
MEMS £3.50
£3 BEFORE 11 P.M.

GOSSIPS.
69 DEAN ST W.1.
9.30 P.M.-3.30 A.M.

THURSDAY
MAY 1st '86

Jehosophats!

GAZ'S ROCKIN BLUES

GOSSIPS.
69 DEAN ST W.1.
ADM. £4. MEMBERS £3.50
GUESTS. £3 BEFORE 11 P.M. £1 MEMBERSHIP BEFORE 11 P.M.
9·30 P.M. - 3·30 A.M.

DAVE TAYLOR
THUR 13TH FEB '86 + THE D.T.s

live

OH, JOHNNY! PLEASE
COME TO GAZ'S
THIS THURSDAY...

BUT SUGAR YOU
KNOW YOU'RE MY
VALENTINE...
OF COURSE I'M
COMIN' HONEY

GAZ'S ROCKIN BLUES

PROUDLY PRESENTING...
the FOREST HILL-BILLIES

WILD 10-PIECE SOUTH LONDON SKIFFLE & JAZZ R&B, SKA BAND

GOSSIPS 69 DEAN St W.1.

ADM. £4. MEMS £3 £3 BEFORE 11 P.M.

THURSDAY 27th FEB '86

9.30 to 3.30

APPEARING ON — THURSDAY MARCH 6th 198...

THE Jivin' Instructors

PLUS

BIG MA-MAGHEE AND THE FAMOUS BLUE NOTE RHYTHM KINGS—

GAZ'S ROCKIN BLUES

GOSSIPS. 69 DEAN St W.1.

ADM. £3, MEMBERS, £4. GUESTS £3 THEN £1 (MEMBERSHIP)

8.30 P.M.-3.30 A.M.

LAUREL AITKEN

ADM. £4.00 MEMBERS £5.00 GUESTS £3.00 BEFORE 11P.M. MEMBERSHIP £1 (FREE BEFORE 11)

WEST-INDIAN FOOD AT THE BAR

SKA & BLUE BEAT, BLUES MOVEMENT
ORIGINAL BLUE BEAT & SKA MAN

GOSSIPS. 69 DEAN St W.1.

THURS 13 MARCH '86

GAZ'S ROCKIN BLUES

live

GAZ'S ROCKIN BLUES

GOSSIPS. 69 DEAN St W.1.

ADM. £3. MEMBERS £4.

GUESTS, £3 THEN £1 (MEMBERSHIP FREE BEFORE 11P.M.)

9.30 P.M. 3.30 A.M.

PROUDLY PRESENTING...
THURSDAY 17 APRIL

the FOREST HILL-BILLIES

TEE-ROO HALT!

GAZ'S ROCKIN BLUES

APPEARING LIVE ON....

THURSDAY · MAY · 29 · '86

BAD MANNERS

AT GOSSIPS 69 DEAN St. W1

ADM. £5
MEMS £4
£3 BEFORE 11 P.M.

8.30 P.M.-3.30 A.M.

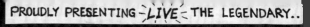
PROUDLY PRESENTING -LIVE- THE LEGENDARY..

GAZ'S ROCKIN BLUES

HUR 10TH ULY '86

LEE (SCRATCH) PERRY & The UPSETTERS

ADM. £4 .MEMBERS.
£5 .GUESTS.
£3 BEFORE 11 P.M. £1 MEMBERSHIP (FREE BEFORE 11)

OSSIPS DEAN ST W.1.

9.30 P.M. - 3.30 A.M.

Z'S KIN JES PS W1

PROUDLY PRESENTS... THE ACES of RHYTHM

THURS 19TH JUNE 1986

JAZZ/R&B FROM THE FORTIES SWINGIN' INTO THE EIGHTIES. HIGH FLYING......

ADMISSION - £4.50
MEMBERS - £3.50
BEFORE 11PM - £3.00

8.30 P.M.-3.30 A.M.

THE POTATO 5

9-PIECE SKA/ROCK STEADY BAND 'THE POTATO 5' 'DEBUT RECORD OUT NOW'

GOSSIPS, 69 DEAN ST'W.1 9.30 P.M. - 3.30 A.M.

THURSDAY 9TH JAN '86

featuring Singer Floyd Lloyd

live

GAZ'S ROCKIN BLUES

ADM. £4.
MEMS £3.50
£3 BEFORE 11P.M.

'SKA EXPLOSION'

AZ'S ROCKIN LUES

OTATO 5 LIVE UREL AITKEN

THURSDAY 3RD JULY 1986
6 YEAR ANIVERSARY PARTY SPECIAL

ADMISSION - £4.50
MEMBERS - £4.00
BEFORE 11PM - £3.00

AT GOSSIPS 69 DEAN ST. W.1

8.30 P.M.-3.30 A.M.

GAZ'S ROCKIN BLUES

RAY CAMPI PLUS SUGAR RAY FORD AND THE HOT SHOTS

9.30 P.M.-3.30 A.M.
AT GOSSIPS 69 DEAN ST. W.1

THURSDAY 24 JULY 1986

ADM £5 MEMBS £4 EVERYONE £3 BEFORE 11:00 PM

GAZ'S ROCKIN BLUES

AT GOSSIPS
69
DEAN ST. W1

APPEARING LIVE ON
THURS APRIL 3 86
R & B FROM ANOTHER GAL-

THE STAR-GAZERS

ADM. £4.

MEMS £3.50

£3 BEFORE 11 P.M.

9.30 P.M.-3.30 A-

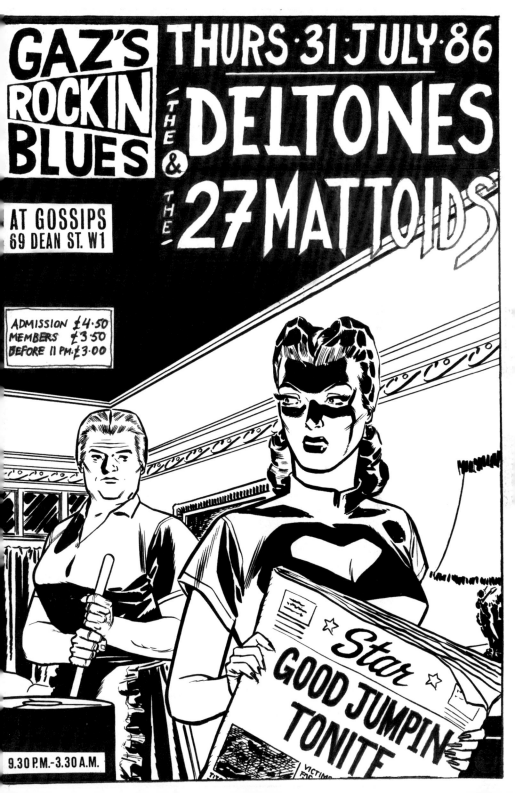

PROUDLY PRESENTING.....

GAZ'S ROCKIN BLUES

CLIVES JIVE 5

GOSSIPS. DEAN ST W.1.

ADM. £4·50
MEMS. £3·50

EVERYONE £3 BEFORE 11 PM

HURS AUG 21 1986

9.30 P.M.-3.30 A.M.

GAZ'S ROCKIN BLUES

PROUDLY PRESENTS

50's **R&B** STAR

Nappy Brown + BAND

Jive with

Nappy **BROWN**

LIVE!

ADM. £5
MEMS £4
£3 BEFORE 11 P.M.

8.30 P.M.-3.30 A.M.

—LEGENDARY VISIT—
DIRECT FROM U.S.A.

THURS 4th DECEMBER 1986

AT GOSSIPS 69 DEAN ST. W1

THURS AUG 14 86

GAZ'S ROCKIN BLUES

VENETIAN GARDENS HOTEL

AT GOSSIPS 69 DEAN ST. W1

HOWLIN WILF AND THE **VEE-JAYS**

ADMISSION - £4·50
MEMBERS - £3·50
BEFORE 11 P.M. £3·00

8.30 P.M.-3.30 A.M.

"I CHECKED OUT THE BOOGIE TAPE, THE STUFF I REALLY KNOW ABOUT, TO GET AN IDEA WHAT THE REST WERE LIKE. IT INCLUDED ALL MY TOP FAVOURITE BOOGIE WOOGIES AND SOME I'D NEVER HEARD OF."

"IT WAS LIKE A UNIVERSITY LEVEL KNOWLEDGE OF MUSIC, SO I HAD TO BUY THE LOT."

JOOLS HOLLAND

APPEARING LIVE! THU

GAZ'S ROCKIN BLUES

FLAG

AT GOSSIPS
69 DEAN ST. W1

ADM. £5 ——

MEMS £4 ——

£3 BEFORE 11 P.M. —

8.30 P.M.-3.30 A.M.

GAZ'S ROCKIN BLUES

PROUDLY PRESENTS..... LEGENDARY ROCK'N'ROLL SAXMAN STAR

HAL "CORN-BREAD" SINGER

FROM U.S.A. + BAND

AT GOSSIPS 69 DEAN ST. W1

RUSH TO SEE HIM FOLKS !!! THIS GUY IS REAL HOT

THURS 27 NOV 1986

-ADMISSION- £5

-MEMBERS- £4

EVERYONE £3 BEFORE 11:PM

9.30 P.M.-3.30

GAZ'S ROCKIN BLUES

DIANA BROWN AND THE BROTHERS SHOW

LIVE!

AT GOSSIPS 69 DEAN ST. W1

ADM. £4·50
MEMS. £3·50
EVERYONE £3
(BEFORE 11 PM)

THURS DEC 11 1986

9.30 P.M.-3.30

GAZ'S ROCKIN BLUES

THURSDAY 16TH OCT 19 86

FEATURING... THE ENIGMATIC...
"MR DYNAMO"...THE DYNAMIC
EMPRESSARIO OF SOUL MUSIC!!
THE MASTERFUL LUDDY SAMMS..
& HIS NEW LINE UP OF SOUL...
DELIVERERS

AT GOSSIPS
69 DEAN ST. W1

PROUDLY PRESENTS —

LUDDY SAMMS

—AND THE—

LIVE!

ADM·£4·50
MEMS·£3·50
EVERYONE £3
(BEFORE 11 PM)

DELIVERERS

GAZ'S ROCKIN BLUES

PROUDLY PRESENTS ON.... **THURSDAY JANUARY 1ST 198**

HOWLIN WILF AND THE VEE-JAYS

AT GOSSIPS
69 DEAN ST. W1

ADMISSION £5
MEMBERS £4
EVERYONE £3 BEFORE 11

LIVE!

9.30 P.M.-3.30

GAZ'S ROCKIN BLUES

THURS JAN 22 1987
WICKED!!

AT GOSSIPS   69 DEAN ST. W1

ADM·£5 MEMS·£4
EVERYONE £3 BEFORE 11

FROM THE U.S.A.
RHYTHM & BLUES
SINGER/GUITARIST
WITH ROCKIN' BAND

9.30 P.M.-3.30 A.M.

BLUES STAR ☆

LIVE!

EDDIE KIRKLAND

Lee Perry at
Gossips, 1988

Derrick Morgan
at Gossips, 1989

GAZ'S ROCKIN BLUES

THU

LIVE!

AT GOSSIPS
69 DEAN ST. W1

ADMISSION £5
MEMBERS £4
EVERYONE £3 BEFORE 11

CLASSIC 60's R&B
+ SOUL SHAKEDOWN
"ROCK STEADY EDDIE'S"
BIRTHDAY PARTY SHOW

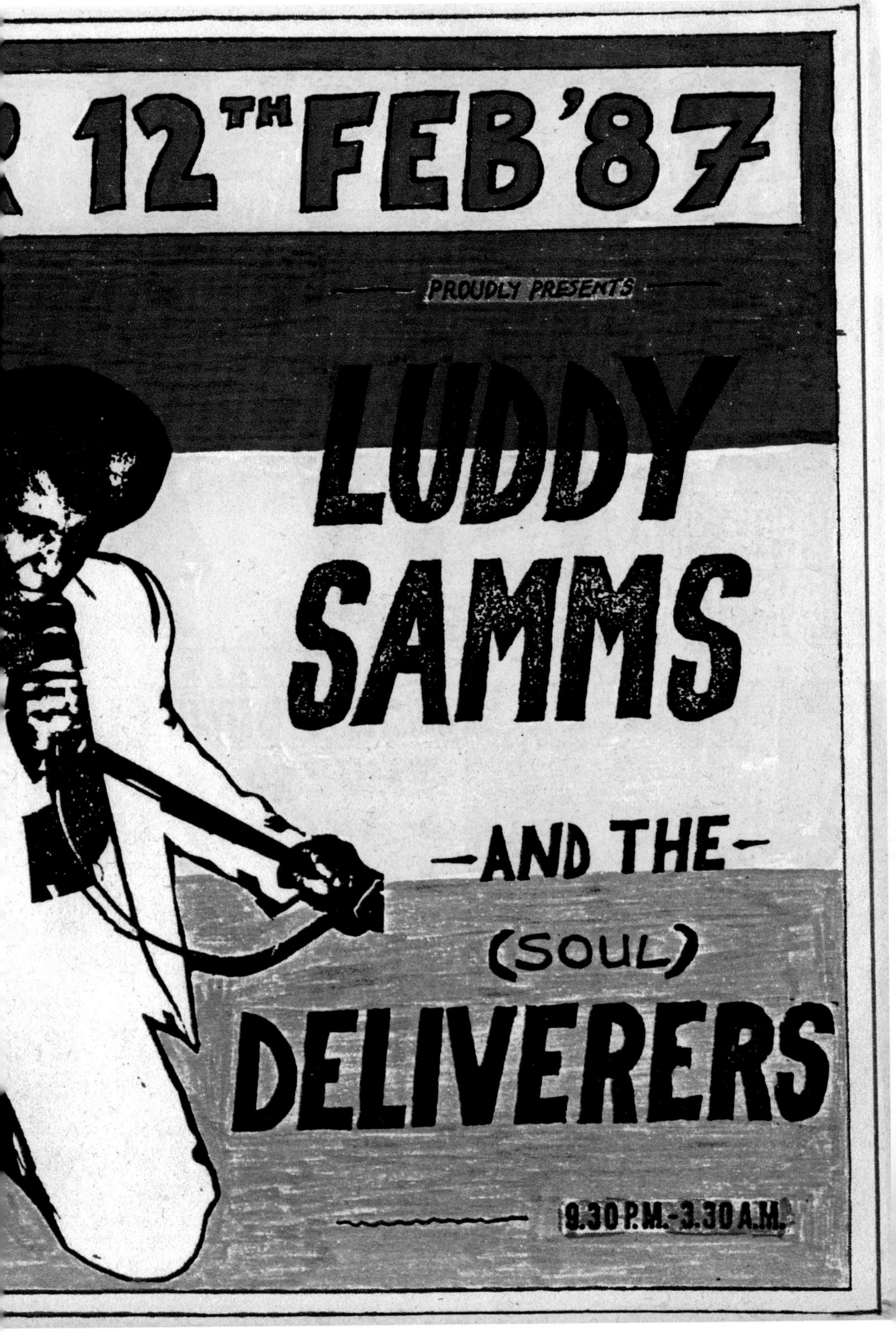

R 12TH FEB '87

PROUDLY PRESENTS

LUDDY SAMMS

-AND THE-

(SOUL)

DELIVERERS

9.30 P.M.-3.30 A.M.

GAZ'S ROCKIN BLUES

THE TROJANS

CELEBRATING THE BIRTHDAY OF JB LENOIR

198

LIVE!

☆ AT GOSSIPS ☆
69 DEAN ST. W1

ADMISSION £5
MEMBERS £4
EVERYONE £3 BEFORE 11

THURSDAY MARCH 5th

9.30 P.M.-3.30

BAR

CHICAGO BLUES REVIEW

THURSDAY MARCH 19th

♫ 1987 ♫

BLUES HARMONICA ACE ◇

CAREY BELL

& ☆ TOP CHICAGO BLUES GUITAR

LEFTY DIZ

STAR PERFORMER ON 1st U.K. VISIT.

WICKED & WILD!!

9.30 P.M.-3.30 A.M.

GAZ'S ROCKIN BLUES

☆ AT GOSSIPS
69 DEAN ST. W1

(FROM THE USA

THE JUNKYARD ANGELS

LIVE!

ADM·£5 MEMS·£4
EVERYONE £3 BEFORE

AZ'S ROCKIN BLUES

IPS. 69 DEAN S'W1.

MISSION £5
MBERS £4
YONE £3 BEFORE 11

LAUREL AITKEN
AND BAND
THURSDAY
APRIL 2nd
1987

8.30 P.M. - 3.30 A.M.

W! L.P. GAZ 001
"Floyd Lloyd & The Potato 5 Meet Laurel Aitken" on GAZ'S Rockin' Records.
RECORD RELEASE DAY PARTY

GAZ'S ROCKIN BLUES

☆ AT GOSSIPS
69 DEAN ST. W1

9.30P.M.-3.30A.M. ♪

ADMISSION £3
MEMBERS £4
EVERYONE £3 BEFORE 11

1987

OUT NOW!

THURSDAY APRIL 9th
The POTATO 5
FEATURING FLOYD LLOYD

LP GAZ 001 "FLOYD LLOYD & the POTATO 5
MEET LAUREL AITKEN" on GAZ'S ROCKIN RECORD

AZ'S ROCKIN BLUES

LIVE!

the Deltones

SSIPS ST. W1

THURSDAY 19TH FEB 87

8.30P.M.-3.30A.M.

GAZ'S ROCKIN BLUES

AT GOSSIPS
69 DEAN ST. W1

ADM £5
MEMS £4
EVERYONE
£3 BEFORE 11 PM

PROUDLY PRESENTS.....

THE QUESTION -AIRES

FEATURING THEIR NEW SINGLE...

THURSDAY FEB - 26 1987.

LOOK OUT!

9.30 P.M.-3.30 A.M.

RS - 4th June '81

Rockin Blues
Gossips Dean St)

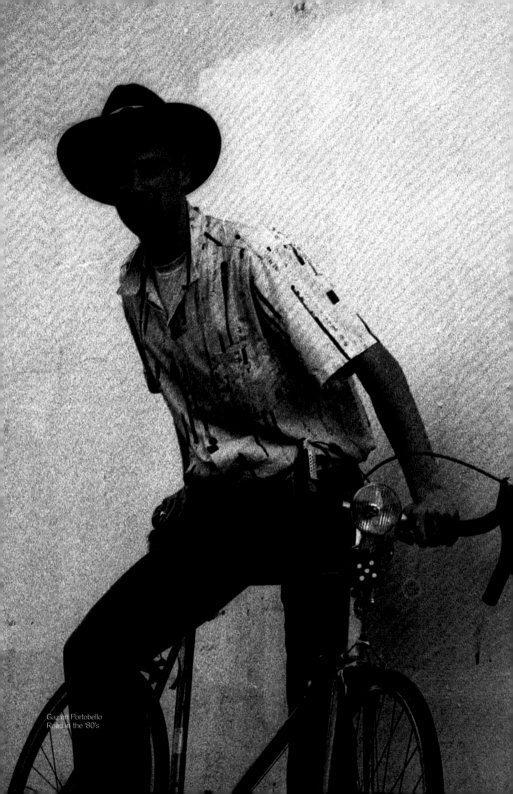

Gaz on Portobello
Road in the '80's

SLEEPY LA BEEF

+ ROCK THERAPY

(FROM U.S.A.)

live at

ROCKABILLY
COUNTRY/BLUES
!! SPECIAL !!

ADMISSION £5
MEMBERS £4
EVERYONE £3 BEFORE 11

GAZ'S ROCKIN BLUES

GOSSIPS.
69 DEAN ST W.1.

THURS 16TH APRIL

9.30 P.M.-3.30 A.M.

'87

GAZ'S ROCKIN BLUES

GOSSIPS 69 DEAN ST. W1

ADMISSION £5
MEMBERS £4
EVERYONE £3 BEFORE 11

THURSDAY APRIL 23 1987

☆ SKIFFLE SPECIAL FROM SCOTLAND

THE HOT LICKS COOKIES

LIVE!

9.30 P.M.-3.30 A.M.

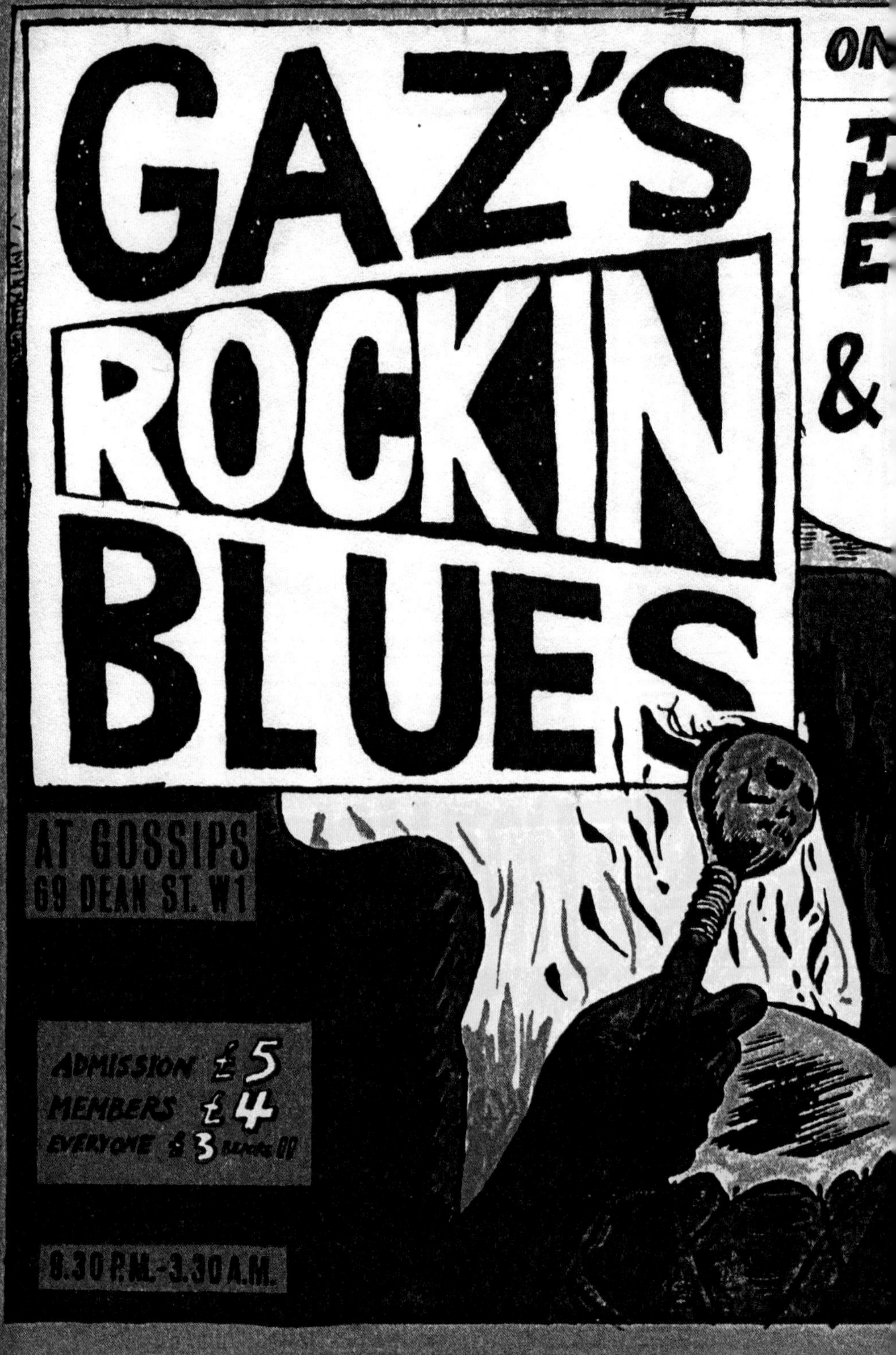
GAZ'S
ROCKIN
BLUES
AT GOSSIPS
69 DEAN ST. W1
ADMISSION £5
MEMBERS £4
EVERYONE £3
9.30 P.M.-3.30 A.M.

GAZ'S ROCKIN BLUES

THURSDAY MAY 7 1987
HOWLIN' WILF AND THE VEE-JAYS

AT GOSSIPS 69 DEAN ST. W1

ADMISSION £5
MEMBERS £4
EVERYONE £3 BEFORE 11

LIVE!

8.30 P.M.-3.30 A.M.

GAZ'S ROCKIN BLUES

DAVE TAYLOR & THE BOOGIE WOOGIE KINGS

AT GOSSIPS 69 DEAN ST. W1   8.30 P.M.-3.30 A.M.

PLUS **THE EMPERORS OF RHYTHM** ROCKABILLY
FROM SOUTHEND...

ADMISSION £5
MEMBERS £4
EVERYONE £3 BEFORE 11

LIVE!

ROCK 'N' ROLL, BOOGIE WOOGIE, R 'N' B, ROCKABILLY

THUR 21st MAY '87

GAZ'S ROCKIN BLUES

THURSDAY 28th MAY '87

Wild!   LIVE!

AT GOSSIPS 69 DEAN ST. W1   9.30 P.M.-3.30 A.M.
Wicked R&B

ADM £5 MEMS £4
EVERYONE £3 BEFORE 11

PROUDLY PRESENTING...

☆ ☆

FROM U.S.A. EXCELLO/BLUE HORIZON RECORDING STAR ON 1st U.K. VISIT

LAZY LESTER & THE JUNKYARD ANGELS

GAZ'S ROCKIN BLUES

LAUREL AITKEN & THE PRESSURE TEN

AT GOSSIPS 69 DEAN ST. W1

LIVE!

THURSD JULY 1987

ADMISSION £5
MEMBERS £4
EVERYONE £3 BEFORE 11

8.30 P.M.

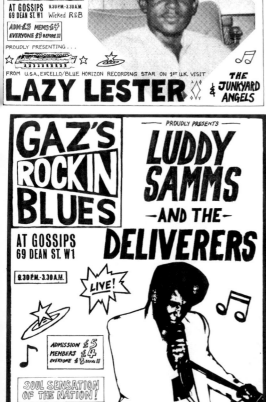

GAZ'S ROCKIN BLUES

PROUDLY PRESENTS
LUDDY SAMMS —AND THE— **DELIVERERS**

AT GOSSIPS 69 DEAN ST. W1

8.30 P.M.-3.30 A.M.

LIVE!

ADMISSION £5
MEMBERS £4
EVERYONE £3 BEFORE 11

SOUL SENSATION OF THE NATION!

THURSDAY 14th MAY

GAZ'S ROCKIN BLUES

THURSDAY 4th JUNE
PROUDLY PRESENTING '8

AT GOSSIPS 69 DEAN ST. W1

LIVE!

ALL-STAR AFRO-CUBA **JAM** JAZZ SWING **SESSION** BE-BOP

FEATURING

LONDONS TOP CLASS JA MUSICIANS STARRING MAURICE CHEVAL

DON WELLER PETE THOMAS ✦ MANY, MANY MOR

ADM. £5 MEMS. £4 (£3 BEFORE 11) 9:30 PM

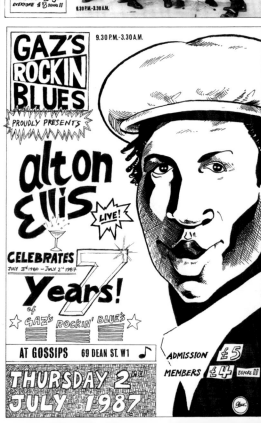

THURSDAY 30 JULY 1987

PROUDLY PRESENTING FROM THE **USA** SPECIALTY RECORDING STAR OF THE **50'S**

JERRY "LIGHTS OUT" BYRNE & JIVE 5

GAZ'S ROCKIN BLUES

GOSSIPS
DEAN ST. W1

LIVE!

ADMISSION £5
MEMBERS £4
EVERYONE £3 BEFORE 11

9.30 P.M.-3.30 A.M.

PROUDLY PRESENTS A
SKIFFLE PARTY
FEATURING | 50'S STAR

THE
CHAS McDEVITT
SKIFFLE GROUP

THE HOT LICKS COOKIES ★

GAZ'S ROCKIN BLUES

LIVE!

AT GOSSIPS
69 DEAN ST. W1

THUR 19th NOV 1987

9.30 P.M.-3.30 A.M.

ADM·£5 MEMS £4
EVERYONE £3 BEFORE 11

GAZ'S ROCKIN BLUES

LIVE!

AT GOSSIPS
69 DEAN ST. W1

9.30 P.M.-3.30 A.M.

ADMISSION £5
MEMBERS £4
EVERYONE £3 BEFORE 11

THUR 10th SEPT

PROUDLY PRESENTING A WILD NIGHT OF CELEBRATING THE RELEASE OF 'LP.GAZ. 002' THE TROJANS 1st L.P. 'ALA-SKA'

THE
TROJANS
'ALA-SKA'

THE
TROJANS

GAZ'S ROCKIN BLUES

THURSDAY AUGUST 6 198

THE M-25

LIVE!

AT GOSSIPS
69 DEAN ST W·1

• • •

ADMISSION £5
MEMBERS £4

EVERYONE £3 BEFORE 11   9·30 AM–3·30 PM

GAZ'S ROCKIN BLUES

PROUPLY PRESENTS...

THE DELTONES

LIVE!

WILD!

AT GOSSIPS   69 DEAN ST. W1

ADMISSION £5
MEMBERS £4
EVERYONE £3 BEFORE 11

— ON —

THURSDAY 20ᵗʰ AUG   1987

— BLUEBEAT PARTY —   8.30 P.M.–3.30

GAZ'S ROCKIN BLUES

FIREWORKS NIGHT SPECIAL
THURS' 5TH NOV 87

T GOSSIPS
9 DEAN ST. W1

LIVE!

ADM. £5
MEMS £4
£3 BEFORE 11 P.M.

9.30 AM - 3.30 PM

THE TROJANS

GAZ'S ROCKIN BLUES

PROUDLY PRESENTS
THURS 15TH OCT 1987

9 P.M.- A.M.

LIVE!

SKA REGGAE STAR

Floyd Lloyd SEIVRIGHT

BACKED BY
RED CLOUD

ADMISSION £5
MEMBERS £4
EVERYONE £3 BEFORE 11

AT GOSSIPS
9 DEAN ST. W1

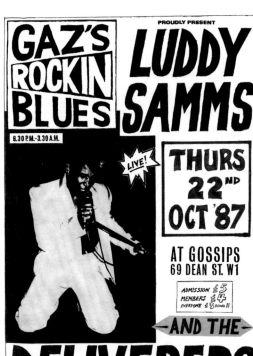

GAZ'S ROCKIN BLUES

9.30 P.M.-3.30 A.M.

PROUDLY PRESENT
LUDDY SAMMS

LIVE!

THURS 22ND OCT '87

AT GOSSIPS
69 DEAN ST. W1

ADMISSION £5
MEMBERS £4
EVERYONE £3 BEFORE 11

AND THE
DELIVERERS

GAZ'S ROCKIN BLUES
LIVE!
THURS 7th DEC AT GOSSIPS 69 DEAN ST. W1
LAUREL AITKEN
ADM £5
MEMS £4
£3 BEFORE 11PM
9.30PM-3.30A.M.
1987

GAZ'S ROCKIN BLUES
BAD MANNERS
AT GOSSIPS   69 DEAN ST. W1
ADM £5 MEMS £4
EVERYONE £3 BEFORE 11
THURSDAY 21st APRIL
9.30PM-3.30AM
1988

GAZ'S ROCKIN BLUES
GOSSIPS DEAN ST. W1
LIVE!
NEW YEARS EVE PARTY!
THURS DEC·31   1987
XII
THE TROJANS
ADMISSION £5
MEMBERS £4
EVERYONE £3 BEFORE 11
9.30 pm – 3.30 am

GAZ'S ROCKIN BLUES
THUR 14th JAN
PROUDLY PRESENTING
HITMAKER
LIVE!
Alton Ellis
ADMISSION £5
MEMBERS £4
FEATURING TOP BAND
UNDIVIDED ROOTS
ROCK STEADY PARTY
REGGAE SUPER
STARRING.. THE LEGENDARY JAMAICAN SOUL SINGER.. ALTON ELLIS
AT GOSSIPS 69 DEAN ST. W1
'88
9.30PM-3.30AM

GAZ'S ROCKIN BLUES
AT GOSSIPS 69 DEAN ST. W1
ADM £5 MEMS £4
EVERYONE £3 BEFORE 11
THURSDAY 10th DEC '87
GOOD ROCKIN JUMP BLUES
LIVE!
STARRING..
Big Town PLAYBOYS
9.30AM-3.30PM

GAZ'S ROCKIN BLUES
AT GOSSIPS 69 DEAN ST. W1
THURSDAY JANUARY 7 1988
ADM £5 MEMS £4
EVERYONE £3 BEFORE 11PM
FOREST HILLBILLIES
9.30PM-3.30

GAZ'S ROCKIN BLUES
GOSSIPS DEAN ST. W1
LIVE!
XMAS EVE PARTY SPECIAL
DECEMBER 24th 1987-STARRING
THE JOE LOUIS BLUES BAND
+ - VERY -! SPECIAL GUESTS
9.30PM-3.30A.M.
ADMISSION £5
MEMBERS £4
EVERYONE £3 BEFORE 11

GAZ'S ROCKIN BLUES

THE GODFATHER OF Ska

PROUDLY PRESENTS

LIVE!

of

LAUREL AITKEN

AND THE

PRESSURE TENANTS

THURS 17TH MARCH

88

AT GOSSIPS
69 DEAN ST. W1

ADMISSION £5
MEMBERS £4
EVERYONE £3 BEFORE 11

9.30P.M.-3.30A.M.

The Cosmics, 1990

GAZ'S ROCKIN BLUES

AT GOSSIPS 69 DEAN ST. W1

PROUDLY PRESENTS

LIVE!

& THE TROJANS

& THE LOAFERS

9.30 P.M.- 3.30 A.M.

COME TO THE MANIC! SKA HEARTY PARTY

THURSDAY 7TH APRIL '88

ADMISSION £5
MEMBERS £4
EVERYONE £3 BEFORE

GAZ'S ROCKIN BLUES

AT GOSSIPS 69 DEAN ST. W1

ADM·£5 MEMS·£4
EVERYONE £3 BEFORE 11

THURSDAY 14TH APR '88

RED'S BIRTHDAY PARTY

Big Town PLAYBOYS

9.30 AM - 3:30 PM

GAZ'S ROCKIN' BLUES   8TH   ANNIVERSARY   PARTY

GAZ'S ROCKIN BLUES

THURSDAY 7TH JULY '88

STARRING... "MR SEA CRUISE"

AT GOSSIPS   69 DEAN ST. W1   FROM NEW ORLEANS, U.S.A. THE LEGEND

LIVE!

FRANKIE FORD

& THE RED HOT POKERS

FRANKIE FORD

ADMISSION £5 ONLY
MEMBERS £4 BEFORE 11

9.30 P.M. - 3.30 A.M.

GAZ'S ROCKIN BLUES

THE WISE MONKEYS

LADBROKE GROVE SPECIAL

AT GOSSIPS 69 DEAN ST. W1

THURSDAY 8TH SEPT 1988

ADMISSION £5 MEMBERS £4 EVERYONE £3 BEFORE 11

SUPPORTED BY SONS OF THE DESERT

GAZ'S ROCKIN BLUES

THUR 2ND JUN

BY POPULAR DEMAND!

HITMAKER Alton Ellis

ADMISSION £5 MEMBERS £4 BEFORE 11

FEATURING TOP BAND UNDIVIDED ROOTS

ROCK STEADY PARTY

REGGAE SUPER

STARRING...THE LEGENDARY JAMAICAN SOUL SINGER ALTON ELLIS

AT GOSSIPS 69 DEAN ST. W1

9.30 P.M.

GAZ'S ROCKIN BLUES

MAROON TOWN

LIVE!

AT GOSSIPS 69 DEAN ST. W1

THURSDAY JUN 16TH 1988

9.30 P.M.-3.30 A.M.

ADMISSION £5 MEMBERS £4 EVERYONE £3 BEFORE 11

GAZ'S ROCKIN BLUES

THURS 23TH JUN

AT GOSSIPS 69 DEAN ST. W1

LIVE!

ADM £5 MEMS £4 £3 BEFORE 11PM

THE TROJAN

9.30 P.M.-3.30 P.M.

GAZ'S ROCKIN BLUES

PROUDLY PRESENTING ON

THURS 12TH MAY '88

ALWAYS HOT

OTIS GRAND & THE DANCEKINGS

AT GOSSIPS 69 DEAN ST. W1

ADM £5 MEMS £4 EVERYONE £3 BEFORE 11

☆☆☆ BIG BAND R AND B ☆☆☆☆☆☆☆

9.30 P.M.-3.30 A.M.

GAZ'S ROCKIN BLUES

DESMOND

LIVE!

THU 2 APR 198

DEKKE

AT GOSSIPS 69 DEAN ST. W1

ADMISSION £5 ONLY MEMBERS £4 BEFORE 11

9.30 P.M.-3.30 A.M.

GAZ'S ROCKIN BLUES

LAUREL AITKEN AND THE POTATO 5

AT GOSSIPS 69 DEAN ST. W1

ADM £5 MEMS £4 EVERYONE £3 BEFORE 11

THURSDAY 5TH MAY 1988

LIVE!

GAZ'S ROCKIN BLUES

THE SKA-TICIAN

AT GOSSIPS 69 DEAN ST. W1

THURS 21ST JULY

LIVE!

ADMISSION £5 MEMBERS £4 EVERYONE £3 BEFORE 11

FEATURING JESSE GREEN

'88

9.30 P.M.-3.30

GAZ'S ROCKIN BLUES

THUR 14TH JULY 1988

— PROUDLY PRESENTING —

GOSSIPS.
69 DEAN St W.1.

U.S. ROCKABILLY STAR ☆

JOHNNY POWERS

WITH THE

PLAYBOYS

LIVE

9.30 P.M. - 3.30 A.M.

ADM. £5 MEMS. £4 BEFORE 11 £3

Johnny Powers

GAZ'S ROCKIN BLUES

THURS 26TH MAY 1988

HOWLIN WILF AND THE VEE-JAYS

LIVE!

AT GOSSIPS
69 DEAN ST. W1

9.30 P.M.-3.30 A.M.

ADMISSION £5
MEMBERS £4
EVERYONE £3 BEFORE 11

GAZ'S ROCKIN BLUES

The Deltones

AT GOSSIPS
69 DEAN ST. W1

LIVE!

ADMISSION £5
MEMBERS £4
EVERYONE £3 BEFORE 11

9.30 P.M.-3.30 A.M.

THU 11TH AUG

PRESENTING FROM TOKYO, JAPAN. 11-PIECE SKA BAND. DEBUT U.K. PERFORMANCE.

THE SKA-FLAMES

GAZ'S ROCKIN BLUES

T GOSSIPS
9 DEAN ST. W1

OMISSION £5
EMBERS £4
ERYONE £3 BEFORE 11

LIVE!

25TH AUG '88

AUTHENTIC BLUE BEAT

GAZ'S ROCKIN BLUES

IPS 69 DEAN ST. W1

RAY CAMPI

PRESENTS A

OCK 'N' ROLL
PLE BILL

SUGAR RAY FORD
AND THE **HOT SHOTS**

SONNY WEST &
THE RHYTHM KINGS

9.30P.M.-3.30A.M.

5 MEMS £4
ONE £3 BEFORE 11

THUR 28TH JULY 1988

GAZ'S ROCKIN BLUES

IPS 69 DEAN ST. W1

PROUDLY PRESENT

LUDDY SAMMS

—AND THE—

DELIVERERS

(60's SOUL SENSATION)

LIVE!

THURSDAY
1ST SEPT 1988

SION £5
RS £4
£3 BEFORE 11

9.30 P.M.-3.30A.M.

GAZ'S ROCKIN BLUES

'Gossips', 69 Dean Street (off Shaftesbury Ave.)

THU 4TH AUGUST 1988

PROUDLY PRESENTING... LEADER OF THE
"MONSTER RAVING LOONEY PARTY" LIVE!

SCREAMING LORD SUTCH

& THE SAVAGES

9.30P.M.-3.30A.M.

DECCA
45-F 11338
JACK THE RIPPER
SCREAMING LORD SUTCH

ORIOLE

WILD 1

ADM. £5   MEMBERS £4   GUESTS

£3.   BEFORE 11 P.M.

MEMBERSHIP £1

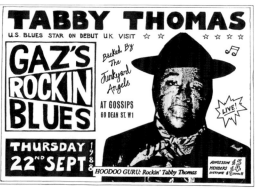

TABBY THOMAS
U.S. BLUES STAR ON DEBUT U.K. VISIT ☆ ☆ ☆   ☆ ☆ ☆ ☆

GAZ'S ROCKIN BLUES

Backed By The Junkyard Angels

AT GOSSIPS
69 DEAN ST. W1

LIVE!

THURSDAY
22ND SEPT 1988

HOODOO GURU: Rockin' Tabby Thomas

ADMISSION £3
MEMBERS £4
EVERYONE £3 BEFORE 11

GAZ'S ROCKIN BLUES

THE HOT DIGGEDY DOG

8.30 P.M. - 3.30 A.M.
LIVE!

AT GOSSIPS
69 DEAN ST. W1

ADMISSION £5
MEMBERS £4
EVERYONE £3 BEFORE 11

THURSDAY
17TH NOV

GAZ'S ROCKIN BLUES

DECEMBER 1ST 1988

THE POTATO 5

LIVE!

AT GOSSIPS   69 DEAN ST. W1

ADM £5 MEMS £4
EVERYONE £3 BEFORE 11

LIVE!

9.30 P.M. - 3.30 A.M.

GAZ'S ROCKIN BLUES

AT GOSSIPS
69 DEAN ST. W1

9.30 P.M. - 3.30 A.M.

THUR 8TH D

SONNY &
THE RHYTHM KIL
WES

PLUS

AMACO
CADIZ

ADM.. £5   MEMBERS
EVERYONE £

GAZ'S ROCKIN BLUES

ADM. £5
MEMS £4
£3 BEFORE 11 P.M.

AT GOSSIPS
69 DEAN ST. W1

THURS
29TH SEPT 1988

THE TROJANS

SUPPORTED BY THE COLUMBIANS

Live

9.30 AM - 3.30 PM

GAZ'S ROCKIN BLUES

THE BLUES-BUSTERS

LIVE

AT GOSSIPS
69 DEAN ST. W1

OM. £5 ——— £3 BEFORE 11 P.M.

EMS £4.

MEMBERSHIP £1 · FREE BEFORE 11 PM ·

THURSDAY
10th NOV '88'

GAZ'S ROCKIN BLUES

9.30 P.M.-3.30 A.M.   AT GOSSIPS   69 DEAN ST. W1

BACK BY POPULAR DEMAND

LIVE!

Y PRESENTS] STAR 'S' MONKEY CHOP

DAN-I & KI

U.K. PERFORMANCE

URSDAY TH SEPT 88

ADMISSION £5
MEMBERS £4
EVERYONE £3 BEFORE 11

APPEARING ON — **THURSDAY 13th OCT**   1988

THE Jivin' Instructors

LIVE!

GAZ'S ROCKIN BLUES

FEATURING ...
THE JIVERS
HOTTEST
LINE-UP EVER

GOSSIPS,
69 DEAN St W.1.

ADM.. £5, MEMBERS £4
EVERYONE £3 BEFORE 11

8.30 P.M.-3.30 A.M.

GAZ'S ROCKIN BLUES

A BLUES DOUBLE BILL!

£5 MEMS £4
YONE £3 BEFORE 11

URSDAY OCT '88

AT GOSSIPS
69 DEAN ST. W1

ROMA PIERRE
& HER
BACK DOORMEN

LIVE!

+ THE
BLUE
RHYTHM
METHODISTS

THURSDAY 20th OCT 1988

THE BIG TOWN PLAYBOYS

GAZ'S ROCKIN BLUES

☆ AT GOSSIPS ☆
69 DEAN ST. W1

9.30 P.M.-3.30 A.M.

ADM.. £5,

MEMBERS £4
EVERYONE £3 BEFORE 11

GAZ'S ROCKIN BLUES

JOE LOUIS BLUES BAND LIVE

ADM. £5
MEMS £4
£3 BEFORE 11PM

AT GOSSIPS 69 DEAN ST. W1

9.30 P.M.-3.30 P.M.

THURSDAY 15th DEC 1988

GAZ'S ROCKIN BLUES

AT GOSSIPS 69 DEAN ST. W1

PROUDLY PRESENTS

LIVE!

COME TO THE MANIC! XMAS PARTY

& THE TROJANS & THE LOAFERS

9.30 P.M.-3.30

THURS 29th DEC 1988

ADMISSION
MEMBERS
EVERYONE

GAZ'S ROCKIN BLUES

AT GOSSIPS 69 DEAN ST. W1

9.30 P.M.-3.30 A.M.

ADMISSION £5
MEMBERS £4
EVERYONE £3 BEFORE 11

SKA-R&B DOUBLE BILL!

SHOUT SISTER SHOUT! & SKAOS

LIVE!

SPECIAL CHRISTMAS PARTY

THURSDAY 22nd DEC 1988

GAZ'S ROCKIN BLUES

The Deltones

AT GOSSIPS 69 DEAN ST. W1

ADMISSION £5
MEMBERS £4
EVERYONE £3 BEFORE 11

LIVE!

9.30 P.M.-3.30 A.M.

THURSDAY JANUARY 5th 1989

GAZ'S ROCKIN BLUES

MAROON TOWN

LIVE!

AT GOSSIPS 69 DEAN ST. W1

THURSDAY JAN 12th 1989

9.30 P.M.-3.30 A.M.

ADMISSION £5
MEMBERS £4
EVERYONE £3 BEFORE 11

GAZ'S ROCKIN BLUES

PROUDLY PRESENTS

THE GODFATHER OF SKA

LIVE!

LAUREL AITKEN AND THE PRESSURE TENANTS

THURS 2nd FEBUARY 89

AT GOSSIPS 69 DEAN ST. W1

ADMISSION £5
MEMBERS £4
EVERYONE £3 BEFORE 11

8.30 P.M.-3.30

GAZ'S ROCKIN BLUES

PROUDLY PRESENTS

LUDDY SAMMS AND THE DELIVERERS

AT GOSSIPS 69 DEAN ST. W1

8.30 P.M.-3.30 A.M.

THURS 26 JANUARY 1989

ADMISSION £5 MEMBERS £4 EVERYONE £3 BEFORE 11

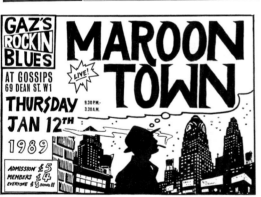

GAZ'S ROCKIN BLUES

OSSIPS.
DEAN St W.1.

ADMISSION £5
MEMBERS £4
EVERYONE £3 BEFORE 11

THURSDAY 19TH JAN 89

PROUDLY PRESENTING

the LOAFERS

LIVE!

NO FIXED ABODE

LIVING SKA & BLUE BEAT,

PRINCE WORTHY

& ROOTS MELODY

LIVE!

THURSDAY 23RD FEB '89

ADMISSION £5
MEMBERS £4
EVERYONE £3 BEFORE 11

GAZ'S ROCKIN BLUES

9.30 P.M. - 3.30 A.M.   AT GOSSIPS   69 DEAN ST. W1

GAZ'S ROCKIN BLUES

AT GOSSIPS
69 DEAN ST. W1

ADMISSION £5
MEMBERS £4
EVERYONE £3 BEFORE 11

1987

THURSDAY MARCH 26
60's SOUL
DOUBLE FEATURE

NIGHT SHIFT ★ THE NIGHT TRAINS

9.30 P.M. - 3.30 A.M.

GAZ'S ROCKIN BLUES

THURSDAY 24TH NOV • 1988

SONS of the **DESERT**

AT GOSSIPS
69 DEAN ST. W1

9.30 P.M.-3.30 A.M.

ADMISSION £5
MEMBERS £4
EVERYONE £3 BEFORE 11

GAZ'S ROCKIN BLUES

10 P.M.-3.30 A.M.

HOWLIN' WILF & the **Vee-Jays**

LIVE!

APPEARING ON —

THURSDAY 9TH FEB 1989

ADMISSION £5
MEMBERS £4
EVERYONE £3 BEFORE 11

T GOSSIPS
9 DEAN ST. W1

GAZ'S ROCKIN BLUES

• THURSDAY MARCH 2 • 1989

GOSSIPS 69 DEAN ST. W1

☆ THE **TROJANS** ☆

ADMISSION £5   MEMBERS £4   EVERYONE £3 BEFORE 11

GAZ'S ROCKIN BLUES

FEBUARY 16TH 1989

LIVE! THE POTATO 5

AT GOSSIPS 69 DEAN ST. W1

ADM £5 MEMS £4 EVERYONE £3 BEFORE 11

LIVE!

GAZ'S ROCKIN BLUES

PRESENTS: ROMAS PENULTIMATE SHOW !!!

ADM £5 MEMS £4 EVERYONE £3 BEFORE 11

THURSDAY 9TH MARCH 89

AT GOSSIPS 69 DEAN ST. W1

LIVE!

ROMA PIER &
BACK-DO

GAZ'S ROCKIN BLUES

AT GOSSIPS 69 DEAN ST. W1

THURSDAY 16TH MAR 1989

9.30 P.M.-3.30 A.M.

little
NORTHERN SKA !!!
Chief

ADMISSION £5
MEMBERS £4
EVERYONE £3 BEFORE 11

GAZ'S ROCKIN BLUES

AT GOSSIPS 69 DEAN ST. W1

9.30 P.M.-3.30 A.M.

THUR 23RD

SONNY & WES
THE RHYTHM KIN

PLUS

THE BAND

ADM.. £5, MEMBERS EVERYONE £

GAZ'S ROCKIN BLUES

AT GOSSIPS 69 DEAN ST. W1

HOTKNIVES

LIVE!

ADMISSION £5
MEMBERS £4
EVERYONE £3 BEFORE 11

THURSDAY 30 MARCH 1989

9.30 P.M.-3.30

GAZ'S ROCKIN BLUES

AT GOSSIPS 69 DEAN ST. W1

THURS 6TH APRIL

9.30 P.M.-3.30 A.M.

ADMISSION £5
MEMBERS £4
EVERYONE £3 BEFORE 11

RAY GELATO'S GIANTS OF

JIVE

THURSDAY 20 APRIL 1989

ADMISSION £5
MEMBERS £4
EVERYONE £3 BEFORE 11

GAZ'S ROCKIN BLUES

AT GOSSIPS 69 DEAN ST. W1

 RED

LEGENDARY US BLUES STAR

LIVE!

8.30 P.M.-3.30 A.M.

GAZ'S ROCKIN BLUES

☆ AT GOSSIPS ☆
69 DEAN ST. W1

THURSDAY
11ᵗʰ MAY 1989

ADMISSION £5
MEMBERS £4
EVERYONE £3 BEFORE 11

BIG JAY McNEELY

BACKED BY THE DAVE TAYLOR BAND

LIVE!

8.30 P.M.-3.30 A

GAZ'S ROCKIN BLUES

AT GOSSIPS
69 DEAN ST. W1

THURSDAY
4TH MAY
1989

THE
TROJANS

LIVE!

ADMISSION £5   MEMBERS £4   EVERYONE £3 BEFORE 11

GAZ'S ROCKIN BLUES

'Gossips', 69 Dean Street (off Shaftesbury Ave.)

THU 8TH JUNE 1989
PROUDLY PRESENTING.. LEADER OF THE
"MONSTER RAVING LOONEY PARTY" LIVE!

SCREAMING LORD SUTCH
& THE SAVAGES

9.30 P.M.-3.30 A.M.

ADM. £5 MEMBERS £4 GUESTS
£3. BEFORE 11 P.M.
MEMBERSHIP £1

DECCA

GAZ'S ROCKIN BLUES

PROUDLY PRESENTS

THE **SKADOW**

9.30 P.M.-3.30 A.M.

ska'd

R.I.P SKANK IN PEACE

for lif

ADMISSION £5
MEMBERS £4
EVERYONE £3

AT GOSSIPS
69 DEAN ST. W1

THURS 15TH JUNE 1989

GAZ'S ROCKIN BLUES

PROUDLY PRESENTS

LUDDY SAMMS
AND THE **DELIVERERS**

AT GOSSIPS
69 DEAN ST. W1
9.30 P.M.-3.30 A.M.

GAZ'S ROCKIN BLUES
9TH BIRTHDAY PARTY
JULY 3rd 1980

THURS 6TH JULY 1989

ADM. £5 MEMS £4 £3

GAZ'S ROCKIN BLUES

9.30 P.M.-3.30 A.M.   AT GOSSIPS   69 DEAN ST. W1

BACK BY POPULAR DEMAND

LIVE!

PROUDLY PRESENTS   STAR OF MONKEY CHOP

DAN-I
& KI

RARE U.K. PERFORMANCE

THURSDAY 13 APRIL 89

ADMISSION £5
MEMBERS £4
EVERYONE £3 BEFORE 11

GAZ'S ROCKIN BLUES

JOE LOUI
BLUE
BAN

LIVE

ADM. £5
MEMS £4
£3 BEFORE 11 P.M.

AT GOSSIPS
69 DEAN ST. W1

9.30 A.M.-3

THURSDAY 27TH APRIL 198

GAZ'S ROCKIN BLUES

GOSSIPS.
69 DEAN ST W.1.

ADMISSION £5
MEMBERS £4
EVERYONE £3 BEFORE 11

THURSDAY 18TH MAY '89

PROUDLY PRESENTING

THE **LOAFERS**

LIVE!

LIVING   SKA & BLUE BEAT,

GAZ'S ROCKIN BLUES

THURSDAY 25TH MAY 19

SONG of the DESER

AT GOSSIPS
69 DEAN ST. W1
9.30 P.M.-3.30 A.M.

ADMISSION £5
MEMBERS £4
EVERYONE £3 BEFORE 11

GAZ'S ROCKIN BLUES

THURS JUNE 1ST 1989

OSSIPS 69 DEAN ST. W1

~ Proudly Presenting ~
FROM NEW YORK, U.S. SKA BOYS

the Toasters

MISSION £5   MEMBERS £4   EVERYONE £3 BEFORE 11

9.30 P.M.-3.30 A.M.

GAZ'S ROCKIN BLUES

AT GOSSIPS 69 DEAN ST. W1

ADMISSION £5
MEMBERS £4
EVERYONE £3 BEFORE 11

SKA SKA SKA

LIVE!

9.30 P.M. - 3.30 A.M.

THURSDAY 29 JUNE 1989

JAMAICA SKA
SKA SKA SKA
SKA SKA SKA

PROUDLY PRESENT

POTATO 5

SKA SKA SKA SKA SKA SKA SKA SK

GAZ'S ROCKIN BLUES

PROUDLY PRESENTS

FROM U.S.A.
ROCKABILLY
STAR...

Mac CURTIS

GOSSIPS 69 DEAN ST. W1

HURSDAY 27 JULY

& THE DRAGSTRIP TRIO

LIVE!

ADMISSION £5
MEMBERS £4
EVERYONE £3 BEFORE 11

9.30 P.M. - 3.30 A.M.

GAZ'S ROCKIN BLUES

AT GOSSIPS 69 DEAN ST. W1

THURS **7**TH **DEC**

THE ELEVATORS

1989

LIVE!

ADMISSION £5
MEMBERS £4
EVERYONE £3 BEFORE 11

GAZ'S ROCKIN BLUES

AT GOSSIPS 69 DEAN ST. W1

ADM·£5 MEMS·£4
EVERYONE £3 BEFORE 11

CAPONE & THE BULLETS

HOT NEW SKA GROUP — FROM GLASGOW

9.30 P.M.-3.30 A.M.

THURSDAY 3RD AUG 1989

LIVE

The Deltones

LIVE!

U 13 JULY 1989

GAZ'S ROCKIN BLUES

GOSSIPS. 69 DEAN St W.1.

ADMISSION £5 MEMBERS £4
EVERYONE £3 BEFORE 11

9·30 P.M. 3·30 A.M.

WOT'S AL'D'RUKUSS... WHOS A'ROMPIN 'N' STOMPIN' IN DA HOUSE BOY!??

DUBLINS FINEST

THE WILF BROS.

THURS 20 JULY 1989

MAROON TOWN

LIVE!

URSDAY G 10 89

SION £5
RS £4
£3 BEFORE 11

LAUREL AITKEN

9.30P.M.-3.30A.M. ADM. £5 MEMBERS £4 £3. BEFORE 11PM.
"LEGEND" ORIGINAL BLUE BEAT & SKA MAN + BAND

AT GOSSIPS
69 DEAN ST. W1

THURSDAY AUG 17 1989

SKA
R&B
EL CUBANA
ROCK STEADY

live & rockin

BLUES
RED
HOT
WILD
REGGAE

GAZ'S ROCKIN BLUES

GAZ'S ROCKIN BLUES

PRESENTS

TABBY THOMAS

THURS 14 SEPT 1989

LIVE!

AT GOSSIPS
69 DEAN ST. W1

ADMISSION £5   MEMBERS £4   EVERYONE £3 BEFORE 11   9.30 P.M.-3.30 A.M.

GAZ'S ROCKIN BLUES

THURSDAY 19 OCTOBER 1989

"I was the highest paid man in Muddy's band because I was the emcee, too." Mojo said. "I could really bring him on . . . 'Ladies and gentlemen, Muddy Missi . . . ssippi Waters!' I loved that old man, he was just like a father to me, and I sure do miss him."

Mojo toured with Muddy off and on until his death in 1983. Mojo's eyes light up when he talks about Muddy. "Been to might near every state with Muddy and overseas five times. Been all the way to Australia."

— "Mojo" Buford

☆ AT GOSSIPS ☆
69 DEAN ST. W1

DIRECT FROM USA WITH BAND

CHICAGO BLUES STAR

MOJO BUFORD

LIVE!

ADM., £5,   MEMBERS £4   EVERYONE £3 BEFORE 11   9.30 P.M.-3.30

GAZ'S ROCKIN BLUES

APPEARING ON 24th AUG 1989

NATURAL RHYTHM

LIVE AT GAZ'S FOR SOME RED HOT VOODOO SKA FROM BRADFORD

GAZ'S ROCKIN BLUES

THURS 7th SEPT

9.30 P.M.-3.30 A.M.

AT GOSSIPS 69 DEAN ST. W1

ADMISSION £5
MEMBERS £4
EVERYONE £3 BEFORE 11

Little PAUL & THE Gentile GIANTS

GAZ'S ROCKIN BLUES

GOSSIPS DEAN ST. W1

30 P.M.-3.30 A.M.

MISSION £5
MBERS £4
ONE £3 BEFORE 11

THURSDAY SEPT 28

THE SKATICIANS PLUS LIVE!

THE RIFFS

GAZ'S ROCKIN BLUES

9.30 P.M.-3.30 A.M.

AT GOSSIPS 69 DEAN ST. W1

ADMISSION £5
MEMBERS £4
EVERYONE £3 BEFORE 11

1989

THURSDAY 12 OCTOBER

THE MERCENARIES

GAZ'S ROCKIN BLUES

AT GOSSIPS 69 DEAN ST. W1

THURS 31st AUGUST

9.30 P.M.-3.30 A.M.

SKA

MISSION £5
MBERS £4
RYONE £3 BEFORE 11

LIVE!

TROJANS

GAZ'S ROCKIN BLUES

AT GOSSIPS 69 DEAN ST. W1

THURSDAY 5th OCTOBER 1989

RONNIE DAWSON AND THE PLAYBOYS

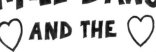

ADMISSION £5   MEMBERS £4   EVERYONE £3 BEFORE 11

9.30 P.M.-3.30 A.M.

GAZ'S ROCKIN BLUES

DERRICK MORGAN

☆ AT GOSSIPS ☆
69 DEAN ST. W1

ADMISSION £5
MEMBERS £4
EVERYONE £3 before 11

THURS
2nd NOV
1989

9.30 P.M. - 3.30 A.M.

TOUGHER THAN TOUGH

BLAZING FIRE

COURT DISMISS

GREEDY GAL

LIVE!

GAZ'S ROCKIN BLUES

AT GOSSIPS   69 DEAN ST. W1

THURS
26TH
OCTOBER
1989

9.30 P.M. - 3.30 A.M.

ADMISSION £5
MEMBERS £4
EVERYONE £3 before 11

GAZ'S ROCKIN BLUES

OSSIPS 69 DEAN ST. W1

THURS 9 NOV 1989

THE JIVIN' INSTRUCTORS

9.30 P.M.-3.30 A.M.

ADMISSION £5
MEMBERS £4
EVERYONE £3 BEFORE 11

GAZ'S ROCKIN BLUES

T GOSSIPS   69 DEAN ST. W1

THURSDAY
30TH NOV

30 P.M.

ADMISSION £5
MEMBERS £4
EVERYONE £3 BEFORE 11

3.30 A.M.

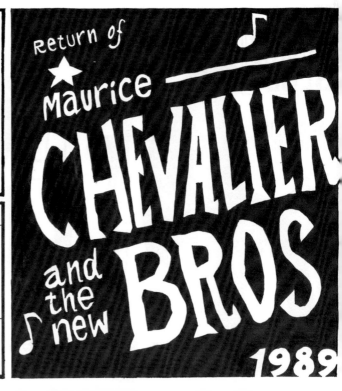

Return of ★ Maurice CHEVALIER and the new BROS

1989

GAZ'S ROCKIN BLUES

AT GOSSIPS 69 DEAN ST. W1

THURSDAY 4 JANUARY 1990

8.30 P.M.-3.30 A.M.

☆ BIG JOE LOUIS ♪ LIVE!

ADMISSION £5
MEMBERS £4
EVERYONE £3 BEFORE 11

GAZ'S ROCKIN BLUES

AT GOSSIPS 69 DEAN ST. W1

THURSDAY JANUARY 1990 9.30 P.M.-3.

☆ ☆

NIK TURNER ALL-STARS

ADM., £5, MEMBERS £4 EVERYONE £3 BEFORE

GAZ'S ROCKIN BLUES

♪ AT ♪ GOSSIPS 69 DEAN ST. W1

LIVE!

8.30 P.M.-3.30 A.M.

THURSDAY — 24 - MAY — 1990

DENNIS ALCAPONE

★ ★ ★ ★ ★

ADMISSION £5 MEMBERS £4 EVERYONE £3 BEFORE 11

GAZ'S ROCKIN BLUES

• PROUDLY PRESENTING •
A NIGHT OF ROCKSTEADY SKA REGGAE PARTY

THURSDAY 16TH AUG
— 1990 —

T GOSSIPS 69 DEAN ST. W1

STARRING

ROY SHIRLEY

FROM JAMAICA
BACKED BY LoToRo BAND!

LIVE!

ADM·£5 MEMS·£4
EVERYONE £3 BEFORE 11

9.30 P.M.-3.30 A.M.

GAZ'S ROCKIN BLUES

☆ AT GOSSIPS ☆
69 DEAN ST. W1

THURS
5
APRIL

9.30 P.M.-3.30 A.M.

'NUFF RESPECT FOR THE MAN CALLED....

1990

DELROY

LIVE! 'DANCING MOOD'

WILSON

— JAMAICAN SINGING LEGEND AND BAND —

ADMISSION £5   MEMBERS £4   EVERYONE £3 BEFORE 11

GAZ'S ROCKIN BLUES

AT GOSSIPS
69 DEAN ST. W1

LIVE!

SWITCHBLADE
PLUS

9.30 P.M.-3.30

JACK & THE RIPPERS

ADMISSION £5   MEMBERS £4   EVERYONE £3 BEFORE 11

THURSDAY 22nd MARCH 1990

GAZ'S ROCKIN BLUES

PROUDLY PRESENTS

LUDDY SAMMS

and His NEW Soul **DELIVERERS** ♪

AT GOSSIPS   69 DEAN ST. W1

THUR 15TH MAR '90

ADM., £5,

MEMBERS £4

EVERYONE £3 BEFORE 11

LIVE!

GAZ'S ROCKIN BLUES

THE SKA! **COSMICS**

LIVE!

THURS 8TH FEB 1990 ♪

9.30 P.M. - 3.30 A.M.

ADMISSION £3
MEMBERS £4
EVERYONE £8 BEFORE 11

GAZ'S ROCKIN BLUES

THURSDAY 1ST MARCH 1990   AT GOSSIPS 69 DEAN ST. W1

ADMISSION £3
MEMBERS £4
EVERYONE £8

OFFICIAL RELEASE DATE OF TROJANS BRAND NEW LP 'SAVE THE WORLD' ON GAZ' ROCKIN' RECORDS

TROJANS LIVE ON STAGE 12.30 A.M.

THE TROJANS

LIVE!

9.30 P.M. - 3.30 A.M.

GAZ'S ROCKIN BLUES

THURSDAY 8TH march 1990

Roots! Ska! from Bradford

Natural Rhythm

AT GOSSIPS ☆
69 DEAN ST. W1

9.30 P.M. - 3.30 A.M.

ADMISSION £5
MEMBERS £4
EVERYONE £3 BEFORE 11

GAZ'S ROCKIN BLUES

☆ AT GOSSIPS ☆
69 DEAN ST. W1

ADMISSION £3
MEMBERS £4
EVERYONE £8 BEFORE 11

THURS 29 MAR 1990

FIRST TIME EVER

DERRICK MORGAN & THE PIRATES

8.30 P.M. - 3.30 A.M.

STEADY   PARTY!

ROCK   LIVE!

RARE U.K. DATE

GAZ'S ROCKIN BLUES

AT GOSSIPS
69 DEAN ST.
W1

ADMISSION £5
MEMBERS £4
EVERYONE £3 BEFORE 11

9.30 P.M.-3.30 A.M.

THURSDAY · 26 · APRIL 1990

THE MOON SHOTS

GAZ'S ROCKIN BLUES

THE HOT DIGGETY DOGS

1990

AT GOSSIPS 69 DEAN ST. W1

THURSDAY 12 APRIL

ADMISSION £5
MEMBERS £4
EVERYONE £3 BEFORE 11

9.30 P.M.-3.30 A.M.

GAZ'S ROCKIN BLUES

AT GOSSIPS
69 DEAN ST. W1

ADMISSION £5
MEMBERS £4
EVERYONE £3 BEFORE 11

8.30 P.M.-3.30 A.M.

THURSDAY 3rd MAY

MAROON TOWN

LIVE!

GAZ'S ROCKIN BLUES

GOSSIPS. 69 DEAN St. W.1.

ADM. £5. MEMBERS. £4.
GUESTS. £3 BEFORE 11

9.30 P.M.-3.30 A.M.

THURS 10TH MAY '90

SONNY WEST & THE RHYTHM KINGS

GAZ'S ROCKIN BLUES

AT GOSSIPS
69 DEAN ST. W1

ADMISSION £5
MEMBERS £4
EVERYONE £3 BEFORE 11

9.30 P.M.-3.3

THURS 17 MA
19

LIVE!

THE PAUL LAMB BLUES BAND

Rock Steady Eddie,
Gaz and Count
Cassavubu,
1995 at St Moritz

The first couple of years weren't easy. A lot of the original crew from the early days had become less frequent visitors over the years. Dom had moved back to Bradford, while Christian had started his own drum'n'bass club and Metalheadz label with his cousin Goldie. Lance and his brother had emigrated to the States, as had Nassa. Last I'd heard of Jim Hall was that he was on the run in Brazil. Josh and Morgan had moved to the country. Most of these guys, including James and Mark Lebon, had now started families. The original kids had grown up but there were some of the old gang still flying the flag, including Count Cassavubu and Rock Steady Eddie, who remained lynchpins throughout the rest of the 90's. It took quite some time until people got used to where to find us at the new address, many assuming that I was still at Gossips.

Similar to my previous residency, St Moritz was a great little Soho basement dive with a lot of history. The club, with a Swiss restaurant upstairs, had been under the same ownership since 1960. Originally a biker's club, it also went through a Skiffle phase. The Kinks played there often in its mod days. It was a disco in the 70's when Joe Strummer's first band, The 101'ers, began playing there. Later famed for its heavy rock nights, Lemmy, from Motorhead, practically lived there for a while. I'd heard glowing reports about that place from Jake Vegas, one of my old guard, who'd run a sleazy rock'n'roll night on Fridays there during the early 90's.

I moved in and began feathering my new nest. I had a new banner made up for the dance floor and put a life-size cut-out of pin-up star Betty Page in the DJ booth. Each anniversary I continued the tradition of putting out bowls of fruit on each table and festooning the place with seasonal balloons and decorations. One evening, soon after opening, an old black guy wandered in just to see if it had changed much since he used to come before the war, when it was a jazz club. He told me it was only the bar room and dance floor areas originally, in those days. When the restaurant moved in next door, they knocked through joining the two basements. He was followed a few weeks later by a group of middle-aged Swiss ex-mods who swore that it hadn't changed since they were last there in 1965.

It was slightly smaller but reminded me of the atmosphere of Gossips in the early years that I was there. Sweetie and Roger gave it a personal family vibe. The wooden beams, tables and bar made it homely. Sweetie, though a restaurateur by trade, was also a musician and party animal, often playing his accordion on tabletops and leading diners pied-piper style on to the street and back again; every Easter never failing to laden all his staff and friends with his specially imported Swiss chocolate. Roger, who manned the door of the club and doubled up as head-chef, was generally very easy-going and popular with the staff and all our friends. Though they didn't chip in towards the bands, they did have a little stage and a built in PA, which was really handy. They had a good line in bouncers, firm but friendly and unintimidating, who quickly got to know who was who. We had JR for many years. When he left to become a pharmacist we got the fabulous 6'6" OJ who's been with us ever since. The cloakroom was situated in one of the two tiny cavernous alcoves at the back of the club. Directly under the pavement, these were originally coal cellars, the building predating central heating by about 300 years. In order to stretch the atmosphere I felt it important to create a wonderful extension of the party. Maintaining a long tradition of having really special girls to man the cloakroom; I can safely say that in the fifteen years that I've been at St Moritz we've had some of the most lovely, bright, interesting, not to mention gorgeous looking young ladies one could have ever have the good fortune to meet holding that post. Actresses Emma and Myfanwy, Belle, Micki, my niece Ruby, my sister Red and more recently Katie and Grace.

As the years passed, we built up a really good scene and plenty of really good bands were soon up for playing there, my own band The Trojans, among them. Having gone through a few changes in line-up, one new guy who joined on percussion in the mid-90's, Natty Bo, soon got involved in DJing. Rock Steady Eddie had got in the family way and followed his life-long dream, moving with them to Ethiopia. In the wake of this, around the turn of the millennium, Natty took over as the main DJ. He left The Trojans to form his own ska band, 'The Top Cats' and went on to form the highly acclaimed 'Ska Cubano', but still finds time to regularly DJ down the club.

Also in the mid-90's, I'd met some cool young kids at a Prince Buster concert in Camden, amongst whom was a very large, red-headed lad with a spiky mohican called Tommy Diamond. He proved to be a top DJ and was keen on all our favourite music.
By the age of 20 he was running the club for me when I toured abroad. Another big help when I was finding my feet at the new venue was the self-proclaimed cartoon gangster, promotor Ska-V-Goldsmith and his Irish mate Russell Kelly, who re-introduced Shane McGowan to the club. DJ Mark Lamarr also helped by constantly plugging us on his BBC radio shows, occasionally popping in for the odd guest slot.

GAZ'S ROCKIN BLUES

THURS **28 JUNE**

AT GOSSIPS 69 DEAN ST. W1

LIVE!

CASINO ROYALE

SKA!

8.30 P.M.-3.30 A.M.

ADMISSION £5   MEMBERS £4   EVERYONE £3 BEFORE 11

GAZ'S ROCKIN BLUES

GOSSIPS. 69 DEAN ST W.1.

9.30 P.M.-3.30 A.M.

THURSDAY 4 OCT

ADMISSION £5
MEMBERS £4
EVERYONE £3 BEFORE 11

1990

Ronnie Dawson and the Playboy

Alton Ellis and
Gaz backstage
at Gossips, 1987

AT GOSSIPS
69 DEAN ST. W1

THE MOONSHOTS

LIVE!

9.30 P.M.-3.30 A.M.

6TH SEP 1990

ADMISSION £5
MEMBERS £4
EVERYONE £3 DOWN 11

GAZ'S ROCKIN BLUES
AT GOSSIPS
69 DEAN ST. W1

ADMISSION £5
MEMBERS £4
EVERYONE £3 DOWN 11

THURS 13 SEPTEMBER

LINDAS BOX OF TRICKS

1990

9.30 P.M.-3.30 A.M.

GAZ'S ROCKIN BLUES

GOSSIPS 69 DEAN ST. W1

ADMISSION £5
MEMBERS £4

1990

SHOUT SISTER SHOUT!

Live!

THURS 27TH SEP

9.30 P.M.-3.30 A.M.

GAZ'S ROCKIN BLUES

9.30 P.M.-3.30 A.M.   AT GOSSIPS   69 DEAN ST. W1

BACK BY POPULAR DEMAND

LIVE!

PROUDLY PRESENTS   STAR OF MONKEY CHOP

DAN-I & KI

RARE U.K. PERFORMANCE

THURSDAY 11 OCT

ADMISSION £5
MEMBERS £4
EVERYONE £3 DOWN 11

1990

GAZ'S ROCKIN BLUES

THURSDAY 18 OCT
AT GOSSIPS 69 DEAN ST. W1
ADMISSION £5 MEMBERS £4 EVERYONE £3 SEND IT
TROJANS LIVE! ON STAGE 12.30 A.M.
1990
THE TROJANS
LIVE!
9.30 P.M. - 3.30 A.M.

GAZ'S ROCKIN BLUES

THURSDAY 25 OCT
AT GOSSIPS 69 DEAN ST. W1
ADMISSION £5 MEMBERS £4 EVERYONE £3 SEND IT
THE NITROS
1990
8
9.30
& JELL SA
ROCKABILLY DOUB

GAZ'S ROCKIN BLUES
ADMISSION £5 MEMBERS £4 EVERYONE £3 SEND IT
AT GOSSIPS 69 DEAN ST. W1
JOE LOUIS BLUES BAND
LIVE
9.30 AM - 3.30 PM
THURSDAY 1st NOV 1990

GAZ'S ROCKIN BLUES
AT GOSSIPS 69 DEAN ST. W1
LIVE!
SWITCHBLAD PLUS THE WELL OILED SISTERS
ADMISSION £5 MEMBERS £4 EVERYONE £3 SEND IT
THURSDAY 22nd NOV 1990

GAZ'S ROCKIN BLUES
AT GOSSIPS 69 DEAN ST. W1
ADMISSION £5 MEMBERS £4 EVERYONE £3 SEND IT
THURSDAY 20 DECEMBER
1990
LIVE!
9.30 P.M. - 3.30 A.M.
featuring THE FANTASTIC
LAUREL AITKEN

GAZ'S ROCKIN BLUES
☆ AT GOSSIPS ☆ 69 DEAN ST. W1
9.30 P.M. - 3.30 A.M.
ADMISSION £5 MEMBERS £4 EVERYONE £3 SEND IT
THURSDAY 6th DEC 1
THE ALL SORTS
SKA FROM THE WIZARDS OF OZ

GAZ'S ROCKIN BLUES
BAR
AT GOSSIPS 69 DEAN ST. W1
9.30 P.M. - 3.30 A.M.
THURS · 17 JAN · 1991
LES PIRES PLUS TIGER LILY & THE JITTERBUG BITES
ADMISSION £5 MEMBERS £4 EVERYONE £3 SEND IT

GAZ'S ROCKIN BLUES
☆ AT GOSSIPS ☆ 69 DEAN ST. W1
ADMISSION £5 MEMBERS £4 EVERYONE £3 SEND IT
THURS 31st JAN 1991
DERRICK MORGAN
9.30 P.M.

STEADY ROCK PAR LIVE!

GAZ'S ROCKIN BLUES

GOSSIPS 69 DEAN ST. W1

ADM·£5 MEMS·£4
EVERYONE £3 BEFORE 11

THURS 8 NOV   1990

100 MEN

9.30 P.M.-3.30 A.M.

GAZ'S ROCKIN BLUES

AT GOSSIPS 69 DEAN ST. W1

1990

THURSDAY 13 DECEMBER

THE TROJANS FEATURING RICO
PLUS ALSO FRESH BACK FROM J.A. . . . . . .

DOMINICK

ADMISSION £5   MEMBERS £4   EVERYONE £3 BEFORE 11

THE TROJANS

P.M.-3.30 A.M.

GAZ'S ROCKIN BLUES

APPEARING LIVE ON

THURSDAY
29 NOV
1990

AT GOSSIPS
69
DEAN ST. W1

 THE COSMICS SKA!

ADMISSION £5
MEMBERS £4
EVERYONE £3 BEFORE 11

9.30 P.M.-3.30 A.

THURSDAY · 24 · JANUARY · 1991

ADMISSION £5 MEMBERS £4 everyone £3 from 11

THE **TOMMY CHASE** QUARTET

NEW YORK SENTINEL — SERIOUS JAZZ

8.30 A.M.

GAZ'S ROCKIN BLUES
☆ AT GOSSIPS ☆
69 DEAN ST. W1

SLIMS CIDER Co

THURS 3 JAN

1990

8.30 P.M.-3.30 A.M.

ADMISSION £3
MEMBERS £4
EVERYONE £3 from 11

PROUDLY PRESENTING FROM J.A.
THE LEGENDARY TROMBONIST

1991

RICO AND BAND

GAZ'S ROCKIN BLUES

GOSSIPS DEAN ST. W1

ISSION £5
MBERS £4
ONE £3 BEFORE 11

HURS · 14 · MAR

9.30 AM-3.30 PM

GAZ'S ROCKIN BLUES
AT GOSSIPS
69 DEAN ST. W1

THURSDAY 21 FEB 1991

BUSTERS ALL★STARS

ADMISSION £5
MEMBERS £4
EVERYONE £3 BEFORE 11

LIVE!

9.30 AM-3.30 PM

THURS 14 FEB 19 91

GAZ'S ROCKIN BLUES

ADMISSION £5
MEMBERS £4
EVERYONE £3 BEFORE 11

GOSSIPS
69 DEAN ST. W1

THE **TROJANS**

P.M.-3.30 A.M.

LIVE!

MAY RED

VALENTINES DAY PARTY!

APPEARING AT The FRIDGE Brixton

St. PATRICKS NIGHT

SUNDAY 17 MARCH

THE **TROJANS**

GAZ'S ROCKIN BLUES

AT GOSSIPS
69 DEAN ST. W1

8.30 P.M.-3.30 A.M.

THURS 7TH MAR

RONNIE DAWSON

★ AND THE ★

PLANET ROCKERS

ADMISSION £5   MEMBERS £4   EVERYONE £3 BEFORE 11

1991

GAZ'S ROCKIN BLUES

AT GOSSIPS 69 DEAN ST. W1

LIVE!

ADMISSION £5
MEMBERS £4
EVERYONE £3 BEFORE 11

KING BIZKIT BLUES BAND

FEATURING DICK HECKSTALL-SMITH!

THURSDAY 28 MARCH

8.30 P.M.-3.30 A.M.

GAZ'S ROCKIN BLUES

AT GOSSIPS 69 DEAN ST. W1

ADMISSION £5
MEMBERS £4
EVERYONE £3 BEFORE 11

9.30 P.M.-3.30 A.M.

THE IGUANA BROTHERS

THURSDAY 11 APRIL 1991

GAZ'S ROCKIN BLUES

AT GOSSIPS 69 DEAN ST. W1

THURSDAY 18 APRIL 1991

LIVE!

THE FRANTIC FLINTSTONES

ADM.. £5,   MEMBERS £4   EVERYONE £3 BEFORE 11

9.30 P

GAZ'S ROCKIN BLUES

AT GOSSIPS
69 DEAN ST. W1

THURSDAY 10TH JAN '91

ADMISSION £5
MEMBERS £4
EVERYONE £3 BEFORE 11

SKA PARTY

MAROON TOWN

LIVE!

9.30 P
3.30 A

GAZ'S ROCKIN BLUES

THURSDAY 25 APRIL 1991

...SSIPS 69 DEAN ST. W1

LIVE!

ADMISSION £5
MEMBERS £4
EVERYONE £3 BEFORE 11

SYCO AND THE NEW YORKERS

9.30 P.M. - 3.30 A.M.

9.30 P.M. - 3.30 A.M.

INNES SIBUN

BLUES EXPLOSION!

...AZ'S ...OCKIN ...LUES

...SSIPS 69 DEAN ST. W1

..£5 MEMS £4
...RYONE £3 BEFORE 11

...URS 12 SEPTEMBER '91'

GAZ'S ROCKIN BLUES

AT GOSSIPS 69 DEAN ST. W1

ADMISSION £5
MEMBERS £4
EVERYONE £3 BEFORE 11

LIVE!

☆ NICK TURNER'S ☆

FANTASTIC ALLSTARS

9.30 P.M. - 3.30 A.M.

THURS 19 SEPT 1990

Return of ★ Maurice

CHEVALIER BROS

1991

...AZ'S ...OCKIN ...LUES

...IPS 69 DEAN ST. W1

...HURSDAY
...th SEPT

ADMISSION £3
MEMBERS £4
...RYONE £3 BEFORE 11   3.30 A.M.

GAZ'S ROCKIN BLUES

AT GOSSIPS
69 DEAN ST. W1

LIVE!

ADMISSION £5   MEMBERS £4
EVERYONE £3 BEFORE 11

THURSDAY 3rd OCT 1991

JACK The & RIPPERS

9.30 P.M. - 3.30 A.M.

GAZ'S ROCKIN BLUES

AT GOSSIPS
69 DEAN ST. W1

THURS
16
MAY
1991

ADMISSION £5   MEMBERS £4   EVERYONE £3 BEFORE 11   9.30 P.M.-3.30

LIKE THIS? WHAT *MADE* ME LIKE THIS? WHO'S TO *BLAME*?

MAROON TOWN

GAZ'S ROCKIN BLUES

AT GOSSIPS
69 DEAN ST. W1

9.30 P.M.-3.30 A.M.

THURSDAY
13
JUNE
1991

SKA-BOOM

ADMISSION £5
MEMBERS £4
EVERYONE £3 BEFORE 11

GAZ'S ROCKIN BLUES

AT GOSSIPS   69 DEAN ST. W1

THURS
20 JUNE

9.30 P.M.-3.30 A.M.

NUMBER 9

LIVE!

ADMISSION £5   MEMBERS £4

GAZ'S ROCKIN BLUES

AT GOSSIPS
69 DEAN ST. W1

ADMISSION £5
MEMBERS £4
EVERYONE £3 BEFORE 11

8.30 P.M.-3.30 A.M.

THURSDAY 27 JUNE 1991
The J·B· FUNK AMBASSADORS

GAZ'S ROCKIN BLUES

AT GOSSIPS
69 DEAN ST. W1

9.30 P.M.-3.30 A.M.

ADMISSION £5   MEMBERS £4   EVERYONE £3 BEFORE 11

THURSDAY 4 JULY 19

TIGER LILY & THE JITTERBUG BITES

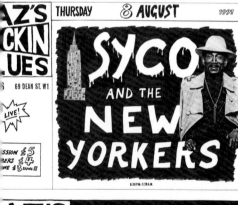

GAZ's ROCKIN' BLUES

GOSSIPS, 69, DEAN ST, SOHO
LONDON W.1.
EVERY THURSDAY
(July 2ND 1980 -?)

11 Years Anniversary Party

FOR FURTHER
INFORMATION
CALL GAZ MAYALL
081-960 4258
(or fax) 081-969 8111

JULY 4TH 1991

American Independance Day celebrations include...

FREE ADMISSION to anyone dressed in Native American 'RED INDIAN' fashion.

FREE ADMISSION to anyone of Native American Indian descent.

LIVE BAND: **TIGER LILLY & THE JITTERBUG BITES**

PLAYING AN HOUR OF CLASSIC LATE FORTIES, EARLY FIFTIES RHYTHM & BLUES
A SEXY SINGER & SAXY SOUND - THREE HORNS, AN UPRIGHT BASS & A GORGEOUS
FEMALE VOCALIST PAYING TRIBUTE TO BLACK AMERICAN CULTURE BY WAY
THE MUSIC THAT INSPIRED ROCK & ROLL, SOUL, REGGAE, FUNK & ROCK etc

FREE PEACHES & NECTARINES

FREE 'GAZ'S ROCKIN' BLUES 11 YEAR ANNIVERSARY' MATCHES........
HOST D.J.'s: GAZ & BEN MAYALL; ROCK STEADY' EDDIE HARMAN, JASON + ASHER G.

DOORS OPEN: 10 P.M.
CURFEW: 3.30 A.M.   NO ADVANCE TICKETS ♬

DOOR PRICES: £3 Before 11 P.M. £5 after 11 P.M. (£4. members)

GUEST LIST FACILITIES FOR PRESS & ANY MUSICIANS THAT HAVE
EVER PLAYED at GAZ's, & likewise anyone who ever worked at Gossips

SKA-BOOM

XMAS STARTS EARLY THIS YEAR

BEST WISHES TO ALL

COME & LETS HAVE A BALL

GAZ'S ROCKIN BLUES

9.30 P.M.-3.30 A.M.

ADMISSION £
MEMBERS £4
EVERYONE £3

AT GOSSIPS
69 DEAN ST. W1

THURSDAY
12 DECEMBER

1991

THURSDAY · 17 · OCT

ZU BOP

LIVE!

1991

at

GAZ'S ROCKIN BLUES

AT GOSSIPS 69 DEAN ST. W1

ADMISSION £5   MEMBERS £4   EVERYONE £3 BEFORE 11

GAZ'S ROCKIN BLUES

AT GOSSIPS 69 DEAN ST. W1

THURS **31** OCTOBER 19

LIVE!

8.30 P.M.-3.30 A.M.

ADMISSION £5
MEMBERS £4
EVERYONE £3 BEFORE 11

TIGER LILY & the JITTERBUG BITES

HALOW
PAR

GAZ'S ROCKIN BLUES

☆ AT GOSSIPS ☆
69 DEAN ST. W1

ADMISSION £5
MEMBERS £4
EVERYONE £3 BEFORE 11

THURSDAY
NOV 21ST

1991

NIGHTCLUBS, BARS, RES
WINE, WOMEN, SONG...AN
LOVED EVERY PRECIOUS

THE BLEACH BOYS

BLUES BAND

8.30 P

STARRING, RICO, JENNY BELLESTA

THE TROJANS AT

ADMISSION £5
MEMBERS £4
EVERYONE £3 BEFORE 11

XMAS SPECIAL ☆

THURSDAY
19 TH
DECEMBER '91

GAZ'S ROCKIN BLUES

AT GOSSIPS 69 DEAN ST. W1

THE TROJANS

STOP ACID RAIN!

In another place, at another time, Chief Seattle of the North American Suquamish Indians said:

"What is man without beasts?
If all the beasts were gone, man would
die from a great loneliness of spirit.
For whatever happens to beasts
soon happens to man.
All things are connected.
Whatever befalls the earth befalls the
sons of the earth.
Man did not weave the web of life —
he is merely a strand in it.
Whatever he does to the web,
he does to himself."

GAZ'S ROCKIN BLUES

THURSDAY 30 APRIL 199?

THE HOT DiGGEDY DOG

🎵 **AT** 🎵
GOSSIPS
69 DEAN ST.
W1

LIVE! | 9.30 P.M.-3.30 A.M. | ADMISSION £5 | MEMBERS £4 | EVERYONE £3 BEFORE ||

GAZ'S ROCKIN BLUES

☆ AT GOSSIPS ☆
69 DEAN ST. W1

THURSDAY
16 APRIL
9.30 P.M.-3.30 A.M.

1992

ASHLEY REID — & the — SAVAGE RABBITS

ADMISSION £5 | MEMBERS £4 | EVERYONE £3 BEFORE ||

GAZ'S ROCKIN BLUES

AT GOSSIPS 69 DEAN ST. W1
9.30 P.M.-3.30 A.M.

THURS • 199?
7ᵀᴴ MAY

LIVE!

EARL SIXTEEN

ADMISSION £5 | MEMBERS £4 | EVERYONE £3 BE...

THURSDAY 9TH JAN 1992

9.30 P.M.–3.30 A.M.

GAZ'S ROCKIN BLUES

☆ AT GOSSIPS ☆
69 DEAN ST. W1

ROCKABILLY!
FROM UP NORTH

THE JUVIES

ADMISSION £5
MEMBERS £4
EVERYONE £3 BEFORE 11

GAZ'S ROCKIN BLUES

AT GOSSIPS ☆
69 DEAN ST. W1

9.30 P.M.–3.30 A.M.

ADMISSION £5
MEMBERS £4
EVERYONE £3 BEFORE 11

THURSDAY 28TH NOV 1991

RED HOT 'N BLUE

ROCKABILLY BLUES   R&B

9.30 P.M.–3.30 A.M.

GAZ'S ROCKIN BLUES

AT GOSSIPS
69 DEAN ST. W1

ADMISSION £5
MEMBERS £4
EVERYONE £3 BEFORE 11

THURSDAY 2ND JAN 1992

INSPECTER TUPPENCE AND THE SEXY FIRE-MEN

SKA, RHYTHM & BLUES, JAZZ FUN
HOT STUFF

LIVE!

9.30 AM–3.30 PM

GAZ'S ROCKIN BLUES

AT GOSSIPS 69 DEAN ST. W1

THURSDAY 16TH JAN 1992

FIRE DEPT

LIVE!

BRITISH BEAT GARAGE PUNK

ADMISSION £5 MEMBERS £4 EVERYONE £3 BEFORE 11

GAZ'S ROCKIN BLUES

☆ AT GOSSIPS ☆
69 DEAN ST. W1

LIVE!

THURSDAY 30 JAN

ALTALAMONT SPEEDWAY

9.30 P.M.–3.30 A.M.

1992   ADMISSION £5   MEMBERS £4   EVERYONE £3 BEFORE 11

GAZ'S ROCKIN BLUES

♫ AT ♫
GOSSIPS
69 DEAN ST.
W1

LIVE!

THURSDAY 6 FEB 1992

DOMINIC

9.30 P.M.-3.30 A.M.

ADMISSION £5   MEMBERS £4   EVERYONE £3 BEFORE

GAZ'S ROCKIN BLUES

THURSDAY
27 FEB
1992

♫ AT ♫
GOSSIPS
69 DEAN ST.
W1

9.30 P.M.-3.30 A.M.

THE TROJANS

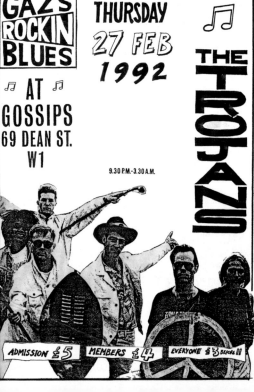

ADMISSION £5   MEMBERS £4   EVERYONE £3 BEFORE!!

GAZ'S ROCKIN BLUES

♫ AT ♫
GOSSIPS
69 DEAN ST.
W1

LIVE!

8.30 P.M.-3.30 A.M.

THURSDAY — 21ST MAY — 1

RICO

ADMISSION £5   MEMBERS £4   EVERYONE £3 BEFORE

GAZ'S ROCKIN BLUES

☆ AT GOSSIPS ☆
69 DEAN ST. W1

THURSDAY
23 APRIL
1992

SUNRISE SUNSET

REGGAE

9.30 P.M.-3.3

ADMISSION £5   MEMBERS £4   EVERYONE £

GAZ'S ROCKIN BLUES

THURSDAY 4 JUNE 1992

CHEYNES PRIDE & JOY

☆ AT GOSSIPS ☆
69 DEAN ST. W1

9.30 P.M.-3.30 A.M.

ADMISSION £5
MEMBERS £4
EVERYONE £3 BEFORE 11

LIVE! LIVE!

GAZ'S ROCKIN BLUES

GOSSIPS
69 DEAN ST.

9.30 P.M.-3.30 A.M.

THURSDAY
11 JUNE

1992

THE SELECTOR

LIVE!

ADMISSION £5   MEMBERS £4   EVERYONE £3 BEFORE 11

THUR

THE
(ORIGINAL)
PR
TH

GAZ'S
ROCKIN
BLUES

☆ AT GOSSIPS ☆
69 DEAN ST. W1

9.30 P.M. - 3.30 A.M.

ADM.. £

MEMBERS
EVERYONE £

MAROON TOWN

AT

GAZ'S ROCKIN BLUES

LIVE!

THURS JUNE 25 '92

8.30 P.M.-3.30 A.M.

GOSSIPS 69 DEAN ST. W1   ADMISSION £5   MEMBERS £4   EVERYONE £3 BEFORE

THURSDAY 2ND JULY 19 92

GAZ'S ROCKIN BLUES

PROUDLY PRESENTS

THE TROJANS

12 YEARS!
ANNIVERSARY
GAZ'S
ROCKIN'
BLUES
PARTY

LIVE!

8.30 P.M.-3.30 A.M.

AT GOSSIPS
69 DEAN ST. W1

BOSS DJ'S
GAZ MAYALL,
ROCK STEADY EDDIE
BEN MAYALL
ASHER GEE

ADMISSION £5
MEMBERS £4
EVERYONE £3 BEFORE 11

GAZ'S ROCKIN BLUES

☆ AT GOSSIPS ☆
69 DEAN ST. W1

THURSDAY 6TH AUGUST 1992

INCESSANT THROBBING

SAVAGE FAITH & the Believers

ADMISSION £5
MEMBERS £4
EVERYONE £3 BEFORE 11

DRUMS...
SERIOUS
NIGHT...

R&B   LIVE!

COME
LET U
GO! I
GETTIN
DARK.

WITH THESE NATIVES!

GAZ'S ROCKIN BLUES

☆ AT GOSSIPS ☆
69 DEAN ST. W1

THE DOWNLINERS ♪ Sect

ENGLAND'S PREMIER GOOD TIME KICK ASS 60's R&B BAND

THE DOWNLINERS SECT

HE DOWNLINERS SECT

LIVE!

20 AUGUST 1992

ADMISSION £5   MEMBERS £4   EVERYONE £3 BEFORE 11

GAZ'S ROCKIN BLUES

AT GOSSIPS 69 DEAN ST. W1

9.30 P.M.-3.30 A.M.

THURSDAY
3rd SEPT '92

INTENSIFIED

PROUDLY PRESENTING

DM £5 MEMS £4
EVERYONE £3 BEFORE 11

GAZ'S ROCKIN BLUES

TOKYO PANORA MA

HAPPY, BABY?

☆ AT GOSSIPS ☆
69 DEAN ST. W1
......

9·30 - 3·30 A.M

~∞~

THURSDAY
24ᵀᴴ SEPT

ADMISSION £5
MEMBERS £4
EVERYONE £3 BEFORE 11

GAZ'S ROCKIN BLUES

☆ AT GOSSIPS ☆
69 DEAN ST. W1

ADMISSION £5
MEMBERS £4
EVERYONE £3 BEFORE 11

THURSDAY
15TH SEPT

FUSANOSUKE

KONDOU

+ HIS BLUES BAND

FUSANOSUKE KONDOU + HIS BLUES BAND LIVE & DIRECT FROM JAPAN...

GAZ'S ROCKIN BLUES

AT GOSSIPS   69 DEAN ST. W1

THURS 27TH AUGUST

9.30 P.M.–3.30 A.M.

SKA

ADMISSION £5
MEMBERS £4
EVERYONE £3 BEFORE 11

LIVE!

THE TROJANS

AAAGH!

HA

'92

THURSDAY 17 SEPT 1992

☆ A NIGHT OF HOT SOUL FROM ☆

BIG VEG

LIVE!

ADMISSION £5

MEMBERS £4

EVERYONE £3 BEFORE 11 PM.

9.30 P.M.

GRR-R-OWL!

GAZ ROCK BLU

AT GOSS
69 DEAN ST.

GAZ'S ROCKIN BLUES

GOSSIPS   69 DEAN ST. W1

LIVE!

ADMISSION £5
MEMBERS £4
EVERYONE £3 BEFORE 11

THURSDAY ○ 1ST OCTOBER ○ 19

SYCO
AND THE
NEW YORKERS

9.30 P.M.–3.30 A.M.

GAZ'S ROCKIN BLUES

BLUE MEANIES

INDIE SKA.....
EXPLOSIVE BONFIRE NIGHT
SPECIAL...

AT GOSSIPS
69 DEAN ST. W1

ADMISSION £5
MEMBERS £4
EVERYONE £3 BEFORE 11

THURSDAY...
5TH NOV
1992

THE DOWNLINERS Sect

ENGLAND'S PREMIER GOOD TIME
KICK ASS 60's R&B BAND

THE DOWNLINERS SECT

LIVE!

GAZ'S ROCKIN BLUES

GOSSIPS
DEAN ST. W1

2TH NOVEMBER 1992

£5   MEMBERS £4   EVERYONE £3 BEFORE 11

PROUDLY PRESENTS...

GAZ'S ROCKIN BLUES

THE CLUB

GREAT YOUNG SKA BAND

AT GOSSIPS

NOV 19
AT GOSSIPS 69 DEAN ST. W1
1992

LIVE!

ADMISSION £5   MEMBERS £4   EVERYONE £3 BEFORE 11

GAZ'S ROCKIN BLUES

RED HOT N BLUE

RELAX JOHN THEY'RE PLAYING ON NOVEMBER 26TH

I CAN'T WAIT THAT LONG!

GOSSIPS.
DEAN ST. W.1.

£5   MEMBERS £4
EVERYONE £3 BEFORE 11

10PM - 3.30AM

1992

PROUDLY PRESENTING.....

GAZ'S ROCKIN BLUES

CLIVES JIVE 5

GOSSIPS.
69 DEAN ST W1

ADM. £5
MEMS. £4

EVERYONE £3 BEFORE 11 PM

THURS 3RD DEC

92

8.30 P.M. - 3.30 A.M.

THUR 29TH OCT '92

GAZ'S ROCKIN BLUES

A SPECIAL TRIBUTE TO THE DEAD HEROS

Andrew Crawford
Byron Upton

THE TROJANS

Confucious
Buddha
Jesus
M. Ali
Muddy Waters
Ghandi

Champion Jack Dupree   Geronimo   Crazy Horse   Louis Armstrong

AT GOSSIP
69 DEAN ST. W

Nick Salter
Don D
Ke
LIVE!
J

Alexis Korner

ADMISSION £5
MEMBERS £4
EVERYONE £3 BEFORE

HAPPY YULE   EVERYONE

GAZ'S ROCKIN BLUES

XMAS

ROCK

STEADY

ADMISSION £5
MEMBERS £4
EVERYONE £3 BEFORE 11

THURS 24TH DEC

PARTY!

AT GOSSIPS   69 DEAN ST. W1   SUPRISE LIVE ACT!

GAZ'S ROCKIN BLUES

AT GOSSIPS   69 DEAN ST. W1

ADMISSION £5
MEMBERS £4
EVERYONE £3 BEFORE 11

LIVE!

THE HIPSHAKERS

THURS 22nd OCT '92

LADBROKE GROVE BLUES

GAZ'S ROCKIN BLUES

GREY COOPER & THE SUN DANCES

☆ AT GOSSIPS ☆
69 DEAN ST. W1

LIVE!

THURSDAY
15 TH
APR '93

9.30 P.M.-3.30 A.M.

ADMISSION £5
MEMBERS £4
EVERYONE £3 BEFORE 11

GAZ'S ROCKIN BLUES

IPS   69 DEAN ST. W1

THURSDAY

JAN

ADMISSION £5
MEMBERS £4
EVERYONE £3 BEFORE 11   3.30 A.M.

LIVE!

Maurice **CHEVALIER BROS** 1993

GAZ'S ROCKIN BLUES

THURSDAY 4 FEB 1993

CHEYNES PRIDE & JOY

☆ AT GOSSIPS ☆
69 DEAN ST. W1

9.30 P.M.-3.30 A.M.

ADMISSION £5
MEMBERS £4
EVERYONE £3 BEFORE 11

LIVE! LIVE!

GAZ'S ROCKIN BLUES

HOUSE OF COMMONS

REGGAE SENSATION

LIVE!

DUB   SOUL   SKA   Blues

AT GOSSIPS
69 DEAN ST. W1

THURSDAY FEB 93

ADMISSION £5
MEMBERS £4
EVERYONE £3 BEFORE 11

GAZ'S ROCKIN BLUES

Katherine **DONALDSON**
stand up comic: live on 25th Feb

OH, JOHNNY! PLEASE COME TO GAZ'S THIS THURSDAY...

BUT SUGAR YOU KNOW YOU'RE MY SWEETHEART OF COURSE I'M COMIN' HONEY

☆ AT GOSSIPS ☆
69 DEAN ST. W1

9.30 P.M.-3.30 A.M.

LIVE!

ADM £5 MEMS £4
EVERYONE £3 BEFORE 11

'93

GAZ'S ROCKIN BLUES

AT GOSSIPS ☆
69 DEAN ST. W1

9.30 - 3.30 A.M.

ADMISSION £5
MEMBERS £4
EVERYONE £3 BEFORE 11

JAKE VEGAS EXPERIENCE
* * *

LIVE!

9.30 P.M.-3.30 A.M.

THURS JAN 28   1993

GAZ'S ROCKIN BLUES

ELVIS DᴬCOSTA
AND HIS IMPOSTERS

LIVE!

THURSDAY
19 AUG ⁹₃

T GOSSIPS   69 DEAN ST. W1

ADM·£5 MEMS·£4
EVERYONE £3 BEFORE 11

REGGAE and
ROCKSTEADY

INKS £1·20
£ 11·30 P.M.

9.30 P.M. - 3.30 A.M.

GAZ'S ROCKIN BLUES

PROUDLY PRESENTING ALL THE WAY FROM TOKYO, JAPAN

THE "SENSATIONAL" 11-PIECE
SKA-FLAMES!

SKA FLAMES

THURSDAY
9ᵀᴴ SEPT 93

ADMISSION £5
MEMBERS £4
EVERYONE £3 BEFORE 11

Sony Records, Japan. Gaz Rockin' Records, U.K.

T GOSSIPS   69 DEAN ST. W1

9.30 P.M. - 3.30 A.M.

GAZ'S ROCKIN BLUES

AT GOSSIPS 69 DEAN ST. W

THURSDAY

1ST APR 93

ADMISSION £5
MEMBERS £4
EVERYONE £3 BEFORE 11

THE TROJANS

LIVE!

9.30 P.M. - 3.30 A.M.

GAZ'S
ROCKIN
BLUES

T GOSSIPS 69 DEAN ST. W1

THUR 25 MAR '93

ADMISSION £5
MEMBERS £4
EVERYONE £3 BEFORE 11

HOMEBOY
BLUES

Katherine DONALDSON

stand up comic: live on 25th Feb

GAZ'S
ROCKIN
BLUES

AT GOSSIPS
69 DEAN ST. W1

LIVE!

R&B

ADMISSION £5   MEMBERS £4

EVERYONE £3 BEFORE 11

THURSDAY 11 MAR 1993

UNDERTAKERS

GAZ'S
ROCKIN
BLUES

☆ AT GOSSIPS ☆
69 DEAN ST. W1

9.30 P.M.-3.30 A.M.

ADM £5 MEMS £4
EVERYONE £3 BEFORE 11

THE
DOWNLINERS
sect

ENGLAND'S PREMIER GOOD TIME
KICK ASS 60's R&B BAND

THE DOWNLINERS SECT

LIVE!

8 TH
AR '93

GAZ'S
ROCKIN
BLUES

AT GOSSIPS
69 DEAN ST. W1

9.30 P.M.-3.30 A.M.

TOO HOT

LIVE!

9.30 P.M.-3.30 A.M.

THURS · 22nd · APRIL · 1993

ADMISSION £5
MEMBERS £4
EVERYONE £3 BEFORE 11

"WHEN ALL THE RETRO CLUBS IN LONDON WERE PLAYING WHITE MUSIC, THERE WAS ONLY ONE PLACE TO GO AND HEAR SOME BELTING 50'S RHYTHM 'N' BLUES AND 60'S SKA."

"THAT PLACE WAS GAZ'S, I WAS THERE ON THE OPENING NIGHT AND STILL LOVE THE PLACE."

JESSE BIRDSALL

GAZ'S ROCKIN BLUES

THURS 12TH MAY 1994

ADM £6 BUT £3 before 11 P.M.

☆ AT GOSSIPS ☆
69 DEAN ST. W1

PROUDLY PRESENTS...

RUBY THroat

STARRING on Lead Vocals... the legendary

IAN DURY + JOCK SCOTT

GAZ'S ROCKIN BLUES

☆ AT GOSSIPS ☆
69 DEAN ST. W1

ADMISSION £5
MEMBERS £4
EVERYONE £3 BEFORE 11

THURSDAY
8TH APR '93

LOONEY TOONS

LIVE!

9.30 P.M.-3.30 A.M.

GAZ'S ROCKIN BLUES

PROUDLY PRESENTING

AT GOSSIPS
69 DEAN ST. W1

THURSDAY
20TH MAY '93

ADM., £5, MEMBERS £4, £3

Council Refugee

SKIFFLE

EVE...

GAZ'S ROCKIN BLUES

AT GOSSIPS
69 DEAN ST. W1

ADMISSION £5
MEMBERS £4
EVERYONE £3 BEFORE 11

THURS 3RD JUNE

9.30 P.M.-3.30 A.M.

Little Willie Complex AND THE INFERIORS

CHICAGO JUMP
MEMPHIS BOOGIE

GAZ'S ROCKIN BLUES

☆ AT GOSSIPS ☆
69 DEAN ST. W1

THURSDAY
29TH APR

ADMISSION £5
MEMBERS £4
EVERYONE £3 BEFORE 11

DOORS
9.30 p.m.-3.30 a.m.
DRINKS
£1 BEFORE 11-30.

THE NEW-MATIC

LIVE!

'9

GAZ'S ROCKIN BLUES

PROUDLY... FREEDOM SOUNDS ... LIVE!
PRESENTING... ...MUSIC MAESTROS...

AT GOSSIPS.
69 DEAN St W.1.

THURSDAY
24TH JUNE '93

ADMISSION £5
MEMBERS £4
EVERYONE £3 BEFORE 11

AFRICA UNITE

♫ GREAT REGGAE ♫

DUB..

ITALY'S Nº1 REGGAE BAND !!

GAZ'S ROCKIN BLUES

ANNIVERSARY PARTY

THURS 8TH JULY '9
celebrating 13 years of...
GAZ'S ROCKIN' BLUES
with special live performance by

JUSTIN HINDS & THE DOMINOES
FROM JAMAICA

SKA/ROCK ST...
REGGAE HERO
FEATURING PAST
LLOYD DELIVERY

GOSSIPS 69 DEAN ST W1   ADMISSION £5   MEMBERS £4   EVERYONE £3

GAZ'S ROCKIN BLUES

~ Proudly Presenting ~
THURSDAY 1ST JULY

ADMISSION £5
MEMBERS £4
EVERYONE £3 BEFORE 11

♫ COLBERT HAMILTON + The NITROS ~ ROCKABILLY BLUES!

Colbert Hamilton & the Nitros

LIVE!

AT GOSSIPS
69 DEAN ST. W1   '93

9.30 P.M.-3.30 A.M.

GAZ'S ROCKIN BLUES

AT GOSSIPS
69 DEAN ST. W1

THURSDAY
27TH MAY '93

ADMISSION £5
MEMBERS £4
EVERYONE £3 BEFORE 11

THE TROJAN

PROUDLY PRESENTING BRITAINS FINEST

BRAND NEW
Out Now ... THE GREAT BRITISH SPL...

12 GAZ 018... BY THE TROJANS IN GAZ'S ROCKIN RECORDS... BUY NOW WHILE STOCKS...

SKA
REGGAE DUB
SOUL JAZZ

GAZ'S ROCKIN BLUES

Proudly Presents

FROM AFRICA THE

DJEMBE DRUMMERS

St. Moritz
159, Wardour St
ho. W.1

m. £6
before 11

Thursday 3RD AUG '95 ← 17TH

Promoting The Trojans brand new record on C.D. & Duble L.P.

STACK -A- DUB TROJANS

Available NOW → C.D GAZ 012

On GAZ's Rockin Records

featuring Prince Buster L.P. GAZ 012

Moritz dour St, Soho

JRS 31ST G 1995

GAZ'S ROCKIN BLUES

at St. Moritz (club)
159, Wardour St Soho. W.1.

THURSDAY 7TH MAR
STARDATE 1996
ADM £6 MEMS£4
EVERYONE £8 BEFORE 11
10 PM - 3.30AM
LIVE!

RUBY: THROAT

GAZ'S ROCKIN BLUES

St. MORITZ CLUB
WARDOUR St. W.1.

£6. EVERYONE £8 BEFORE 11

R 18TH APRIL

PRESENTS THE 30'S
PO·CRACKER

LIGHT? SURE! HERE Y'ARE! ER...CAN I BUY YOU A DRINK?

WHY, THANKS, MISTER! NICE OF YOU! I'LL HAVE ANOTHER OF THESE...

GAZ'S ROCKIN BLUES

ST MORITZ CLUB at
159 WARDOUR STREET, SOHO

ADM: £6. (£3 B4 11). 10 - 3.30AM

THURSDAY JUNE 20

LUNATIC FUNK

GAZ'S ROCKIN BLUES

THE GODFATHER OF Ska

PROUDLY PRESENTS

LIVE!

LAUREL AITKEN AND FREETOWN

THURS 25TH JULY '96

St Moritz, 159 WARDOUR St SOHO. W.1.

ADMISSION £7
Come Early!
EVERYONE £5 BEFORE 11

10 PM 3.30 A.M.

1966   1996

JC 001

World's Fastest Poet!

Birthday Party
Live Midnite Jam / DJ / Band

GAZ'S ROCKIN BLUES

"St Moritz" 159 Wardour St
Thursday 15th August
9.30 - 2.30
Admission £7 (£5 b4 11)

GAZ'S ROCKIN BLUES

LIVE

St Moritz, 159 WARDOUR St SOHO. W.1.

ADMISSION £7
Come Early!
EVERYONE £5 BEFORE 11

THU 22 AUG '96

THE BEETROOTS

GAZ'S ROCKIN BLUES

HALLOWEEN "FANCY DRESS" PARTY

St Moritz club
159, WARDOUR St
SOHO. W.1.

PROUDLY PRESENTING FROM J.A.
THE LEGENDARY TROMBONIST...

RICO & BAND

PLUS · SUPRISE · SPECIAL GUESTS

LIVE!

RICO

ADMISSION £7
Come Early!
EVERYONE £5 BEFORE 11

THURSDAY 31st OCT 1996

GAZ'S ROCKIN BLUES

PRESENTS

live

GNS. N° 1 BLUESDANCE

TROJANS

SAVE THE WORLD... SPIRIT OF ADVENTURE
COOL RULERS
ALA-SKA
WICKED WILD
SKA ALTITUDE · CELTIC SKA
REBEL · SKA... STACK
HAPPY XMAS!! 2
TROJAN WARRIORS... FOR YOUR PROTECTION... THE BEST OF
WILD & FREE

ON THURSDAY 12TH OF DECEMBER

AT ST MORITZ WARDOUR STREET

£7. or £5 B4 11

GAZ'S ROCKIN BLUES

St. MORITZ CLUB
159, WARDOUR St. W1

THURS 6TH JUNE

ADM. £6   10-3.30 am

THE BEETROOTS

GAZ'S ROCKIN BLUES

PRESENTS... LIVE FUNKY BAND

LUNATIC SOUNDS FROM ANOTHER WORLD!

St. Moritz 159. WARDOUR St SOHO. W.1.

ADM £7 £5 BEFORE 11

THURS JAN 2

GAZ'S ROCKIN BLUES

PROUDLY PRESENTS

DAN·I & The Roots SYNDICATE

St MORITZ 159 Wardour St Soho. London. W.1.

ADM...£7 or B4 11 £5

THURS 9TH JAN 1997

GAZ'S ROCKIN BLUES

PRESENTS

L.S. DIEZEL LIVE!

SUB-SIDE... SUICIDAL DUB ROUND THE BEND

LSDIEZEL

St MORITZ 159, Wardour St Soho. London. W.1.

ADM·£7 come early EVERYONE £5 BEFORE 11

THURS JAN 30TH 1997

DOORS 10 P.M. CURFEW 3-30

"SUICIDAL DUB"

RECORD LAUNCH.. PARTY

GAZ'S ROCKIN BLUES

MIND GAP TRILO

St MORITZ club 159, WARDOUR St. W1

ADM...£7 or B4 11 £5

THURSDAY 27 FEB 1997

GAZ'S ROCKIN BLUES

THE BEET ROOTS

LIVE!

THE BEETROOTS

St MORITZ 159, Wardour St Soho. London. W.1.

DOORS 10 P.M. CURFEW 3-30 A.M.

THUR 24 OCT 1996

GAZ'S ROCKIN BLUES

AT St MORITZ 159, Wardour St Soho, London, W.1.

Admission £7 come early EVERYONE £5 BEFORE 11

PROUDLY PRESE A NIGHT OF ROCK SKA REGGAE P

DOORS 10 P.M. CURF

THE TROJAN

6.30 P.M.-3.30 A.M.

THURS 7 NOV 19

GAZ'S ROCKIN BLUES

PROUDLY PRESENTS

WEST ROW

ADM·£7 come early EVERYONE £5 BEFORE 11

LIVE!

St MORITZ 159, Wardour St Soho, London, W.1.

APPEARING ON

DOORS 10 P.M. CURFEW 3-30

THURSDAY 14TH NOV 1996

GAZ'S ROCKIN BLUES

APPEARING ON· 28TH NOV 1

BABAYAGO

St Moritz 159. WARDOUR St SOHO. W.1.

ADM. £7 £5 B4 11 P.M.

DOORS 10 P.M. CURFEW 3-30

GAZ'S ROCKIN BLUES

☆ AT GOSSIPS ☆
69 DEAN ST. W1

1993

ADMISSION £5
MEMBERS £4
EVERYONE £3 BEFORE 11

EVERY THURSDAY

D.J's GAZ,
ROCK STEADY EDDIE,
Count Cassavubu + BEN MAYALL

9.30 – 3.30

FEATURING  LIVE BANDS

Nov 11th – CRAZY BEAT DEMONS

Nov 25th – COOL GREY FIVES (Ro)

Dec 2nd – 100 MEN + Special Guests

(Ska) (Sou)

Dec 9th – SQUINTY BACKBONE
with T. CHEST BASS, VIOLIN
FOR THE FOLK

Dec 23rd –  **THE TROJANS**

7 YEARS ANNIVERSARY

PROUDLY PRESENTING: SPECIAL GUEST STARS; DOMINIC, JENNY BELLESTAR + Manymo

⊘ TALK AROUND SERIES

GAZ MAYALL DJ SHOW

4 / 18（SUN）3：00PM〜

当日、下記の商品を渋谷ＣＤぴあでお買い上げの方の中から抽選で３０名様にＧＡＺ ＭＡＹＡＬＬサイン入り
プロモーション７インチシングル（非売品）をプレゼント。

PRINCE BUSTER
KING OF SKA

JUMP WITH JOEY
GENERATIONS UNITED.

JUMP WITH JOEY
SKA-BA

SPECIALS,THE BEAT,2
THE SOUND OF SKA

【お問い合わせ】渋谷ＣＤぴあ　　03（3499）5028
　　　　　　　　　　　　　　　　ＪＲ渋谷駅東口から徒歩５分
　　　　　　　　　　　　　　　　火曜定休

GAZ'S ROCKIN BLUES

DJ GAZ MAYALL
FROM LONDON
IHARA AND CLUB SKA DJs

94
1.6 **THU**
PM9:00—
¥2500

DJ·BAR
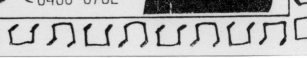
3496-0782

GREAT VALUE

WELL SHAKE IT UP BABY!!

GAZ ROCKIN' BLUES

DJ GAZ MAYALL
from LONDON
NAOKI / NAKAMURA
HIROSHI / MAKINO
from KOOL & FUNK

4 01 08 (SAT) 9:00 START
at SPACE LANDMARK
082-542-1751

ADD 3500
DAY 4000

INFOMATION 082-245-0314 CHAOS

ENDARY

ANS

NIVERSARY ♥

PEC 1996 cc

ADISE

N • 19 KILBURN LANE

2 B4 9PM

Paradise
by way of Kensal Green

THE TROJANs

Wed 31st Aug 1994

Lucky Petes Birtday Party

Doors: 8 P.M.

Entrance: £4.

19 KILBURN LANE W10 TEL: 081 969 0098

Paradise
by way of Kensal Green

Proudly Presents   A Wild! Tues 31st Oct.

HALLOWEEN
party   featuring Live

THE TROJANS

+ D.J's from the area

Admission £5

Concessions £3
(students, O.A.P's)

Everyone £3 before 9 p.m.

Doors open 7.30. close 11.30

19 KILBURN LANE W10 TEL: 081 969 0098

CELTIC SKA

THE TROJANS

OUT NOW !

1st press GREEN Vinyl

LP GAZ 011
CD GAZ 011

Release Day: 5. 12. 94
on Gaz's Rockin' Records

THURSDAY 9TH FEB 95

PROUDLY PRESENTS . . . . .

MEDICINE

GAZ'S ROCKIN BLUES

SHACK

10 PIECE FUNK BAND FROM COVENTRY

LIVE!

ADM £6
MEMBERS £5
£3 before 11pm

ST MORITZ
159 Wardour Street.

1995 RUBY THROAT

FEATURING THE LEAD VOCALS OF IAN DURY

GAZ'S ROCKIN BLUES

MORITZ 159 WARDOUR

£6 MEMS £5
EVERYONE £8 before 11:00

THURS 20TH APR

PRESENTING THE FIRST ROBO-VOX

GAZ'S ROCKIN BLUES

ST MORITZ
159 WARDOUR STREET
ADMISSION £6
EVERYONE £3 B4 11
DOORS OPEN
10PM — 3.30AM

ANIVERSARY

15 YEARS
★★★

SEMI-ACOUSTIC LIVE SET BY

MORIS TEPPER

OF CPT BEEFHEART/TOM WAITS FAME

MUSIC IS THE

PARRTY

FOOD OF LOVE

THURS 6TH JULY

THURS 10TH AUG '95
JASON MAYALL'S BIRTHDAY

CUMBIA PARTY SPECIAL

featuring live from Colombia Filipé Romero

GAZ'S ROCKIN BLUES

Moritz
Wardour St.
W.1.
£6.
before 11pm
10 PM
3.30.

GAZ'S ROCKIN BLUES

at St. Moritz
159, Wardour St
Soho. W.1

Adm. £6
£3 before 11

LEAPING INTO THE LEAP YEAR IN 'LEAPS & BOUNDS' WITH A LIVE SET FROM . . .

THE TROJANS

Thursday 29TH FEB 1996

SKA EXPLOSION '95

おめでとうスカタライツ30周年

LIVE ≡ THE "WORLD FAMOUS"

SKATALITES
TOMMY McCOOK, ROLAND ALPHONSO, LLOYD KNIBBS, BREVETT...

THE TROJANS
GAZ MAYALL, RUDY JONES, KID ROLLINS, ZORAD et al...

SKA FLAMES
NIPPON'S ICHI BAN AUTHENTIC SKA ~ REGGAY BAND...

ILLUSTRATION: GAZ MAYALL

スカ・エクスプロージョン'95
ACT:スカタライツ、トロージャンズ、スカフレイムス(5/28のみ)

5/28 SUN. 東京・日比谷野外音楽堂
お問合わせ:スマッシュ03-3444-6751 ホットスタンプ03-5820-9999 チケット発売 チケットセゾン03-5990-9999 チケットぴあ03-5237-9999

5/30 TUE. 名古屋クラブクアトロ
お問合わせ:名古屋クラブクアトロ052-264-8211 チケット発売 チケットセゾン052-290-0290 チケットぴあ052-320-9999

5/31 WED. 大阪・心斎橋クラブクアトロ
お問合わせ:大阪・心斎橋クラブクアトロ06-211-8631 チケット発売 チケットセゾン06-363-9999 チケットぴあ06-363-9999

主催:TBS RADIO (5/28のみ) 企画制作:スマッシュ/(株)パルコ/ホットスタッフ 協力:クアトロ・レーベル/東芝EMI(株)

PARCO

SKAだけがトロージャンズのルーツじゃない

パンク、R&B、トロージャンズのルーツ・サウンド満載のNEW ALBU

THE TROJANS Rebel Blue
QTCY-2031 ¥2700(税込) NOW ON SALE

REBEL BLUES

ギャズ・メイオール最初のバンド "REBEL BLUES ROCKERS" の、初期パンクから、父親(ジョン・メイオール)そしてハーモニカやパイプを加えた現在のトロージャンズの音楽ルーツ集大成。ギャズそしてトロージャンズの音楽ルーツのスタイルまで、ギャズそしてトロージャンズの音楽ルーツ集大成。

PARCO OFFICE 03 3770 4660 CONVERSATION OFFICE 03 3219 7
DISTRIBUTED BY NIPPON COLUMBIA CO., LTD.

QUATTRO LABEL

THURS

14TH DECEMBER

CHESTER KAMEN'S BAND

LIVE!

at St. Moritz
159, Wardour St
Soho. W.1

Adm. £6
£3 before 11

GAZ'S ROCKIN BLUES

doors 10 pm.
close 3.30 am

GAZ'S ROCKIN BLUES

THUR 28TH DEC.

at St. Moritz
159, Wardour St
Soho. W.1

Adm. £6
£3 before 11

COME TO GAZ'S BIRTHDAY PARTY!

FEATURING

LIVE! **THE TROJANS**

10 PM - 3.3

GAZ'S ROCKIN BLUES

FILIPE ROMERO & LOS PORROS

Live

St. MORITZ
159, Wardour St
Soho, London, W.1.

ADMISSION £7
Come Early!
EVERYONE £5 before 11

CUMBIA FROM COLOMBIA!
WICKED SESSION

THUR 19TH SEPT 1996

DOORS 10 P.M.
CURFEW 3.30 A.M.

GAZ'S ROCKIN BLUES

A Stack -A- DUB

at St. Moritz
159, Wardour St
Soho. W.1

Adm. £6
£3 before 11

Evie's Birthday Party!

THE TROJAN

Thurs 19TH Oct

GAZ'S ROCKIN BLUES

St. Moritz
159, Wardour S,
SOHO. W.1.

ADMISSION £7
Come Early!
EVERYONE £5 before 11

JULY · 18

Come this Thursday to see THE...

BACKBEATS

Live

GAZ'S ROCKIN BLUES

at St. Moritz
159, Wardour St. W.1.

THUR 27 JUNE
10 - 3.30 A.M.
ADM £6. £3 B4 11 P.M.

SYCO & THE N... YOR...

GAZ'S ROCKIN BLUES

at St MORITZ
159, Wardour St
Soho, London, W.1.

THURS 13TH JUNE '96

ADM £6
(£3 BEFORE 11)

COLONEL HATHI

'IT TAKES TWO TO TANGO...
TOO TOOT ANGO...'

RATTLE RATTLE

TOP SKA FROM CAMBRIDGE

DOORS 10 PM → 3·30 A.M.

GAZ'S ROCKIN BLUES

St. MORITZ club
159, WARDOUR St. W1

THURS 6TH JUNE

ADM £6   before ...   10-3.30 A.M.

THE BEETROOTS

GAZ'S ROCKIN BLUES

at St. Moritz
159, Wardour St
~ Soho, W.1 ~

ADM £6
£3 Before 11 PM

THURSDAY
11 JULY

TOO MANY CROOP

BRIGHTONS TOP SKA BAND LIVE

MIND GAP TRILOGY ♪

GAZ'S ROCKIN BLUES
MORITZ CLUB, WARDOUR St. W1
...£7 £5
THURSDAY MAY 97

GAZ'S ROCKIN BLUES

LUNATIC

St MORITZ CLUB at: 159 WARDOUR STREET, SOHO

ADM: £7 (£5 B4 11). 10-3.30AM

THURSDAY MAY 15

LIVE FUNK

GAZ'S ROCKIN BLUES

PROUDLY PRESENTS

The Lorelei

Wild Picts frae Aberdeen

Live Scots

ST MORITZ 159 WARDOUR STREET

DM £7 come early
EVERYONE £5 BEFORE 11

RS 22ND MAY 97

GAZ'S ROCKIN BLUES

THE VIBRATIONS

St Moritz 159, WARDOUR St SOHO. W.1.

ADMISSION £7 Come Early! EVERYONE £5 BEFORE 11

THURS 29TH MAY '97

10PM 3.30AM

GAZ'S ROCKIN BLUES
No 1 BLUESDANCE

THE XPLOSIONS!

Moritz 1. WARDOUR St SOHO. W.1.

£7 come Early
ONE £5 BEFORE 11

URS 5TH JUN '97

SKA! ROCK STEADY REGGAE

WOTS AL'D'RUKUSS... WHOS A'ROMPIN 'N 'STOMPIN' IN DA HOUSE BOY!??

GAZ'S ROCKIN BLUES

St MORITZ 159, WARDOUR St Soho, London, W.1.

Adm. £7 ... £5 B411

DUBLINS FINEST!

THE OTHER BROS.

THURS 12 JUNE 1997

THE BIONICS

Live
Authentic SKA - 60's Reggae

GREAT VALUE

ADMISSION £7
Come Early!
EVERYONE £5 before 11

GAZ'S ROCKIN BLUES

St MORITZ 159, Wardour St, London, W.1.

THURSDAY JUNE '97

10 P.M. CURFEW 3-30 A.M.

WELL SHAKE IT UP BABE!!

GAZ'S ROCKIN BLUES

St MORITZ 159, Wardour St Soho, London, W.1.

THURS 10TH JUL 1997 .... new L.P... "Earth First!

ADM. £7...£5 B4 11PM

FEATURING

THE TROJANS

LIVE!

CD GAZ 015

GAZ'S ROCKIN BLUES

2ND JUNE 1994 AT GAZ'S

THE TROJA...

AT GOSSIPS   69 DEAN ST. W1

ADM £6   MEMS £4
EVERYONE £3 BEFORE 11

THURS 2ND JUN

SPIRIT OF ADVENTURE

TROJANS 1994

GAZ'S ROCKIN BLUES

LONDONS N° 1 BLUESDANCE

REBEL LION

Live

St Moritz
159. WARDOUR St
SOHO. W.1.

THURS 24TH JULY 1997

ADM·£7 EVERYONE £5 BEFORE 11

GAZ'S ROCKIN BLUES

THURS 26TH JUN

AT ST MORITZ CLUB, 159. Wardour St, Soho, Lon

10 PM.- 3·30

LIVE!

ARTHUR K AND THE ORIGINA

SOOTY IS A RUDIE

SKA

ADM £5 BE

GAZ'S ROCKIN BLUES

ST MORITZ
159. Wardour St
Soho. London. W.1.

ADM...£7
or B4 11 £5

THURSDAY
17TH APRIL

Launch party 4 new L.P... "Earth First!

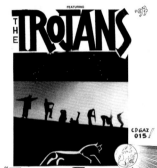

FEATURING

THE TROJANS '97

CD GAZ 015

GAZ'S ROCKIN BLUES

ST MORITZ
159 WARDOUR STREET

ADM·£7 come Early
EVERYONE £5 BEFORE 11

THURSDAY
13TH MAR 97

LIVE!

JC OO

World's
Fastest
Poet!

10-

GAZ'S ROCKIN BLUES

LONDONS N° 1 BLUESDANCE

St Moritz
159. WARDOUR St
SOHO. W.1.

ADM·£7 come Early
EVERYONE £5 BEFORE 11

THURS 21ST AUG '97

TARANTISM

GAZ'S ROCKIN BLUES

LONDONS N° 1 BLUESDANCE

St Moritz
159. WARDOUR St
SOHO. W.1.

ADM·£7 come Early
EVERYONE £5 BEFORE 11

THE TROJANS

Earth First!

THUR 28 AUG '97

new L.P...

SKA

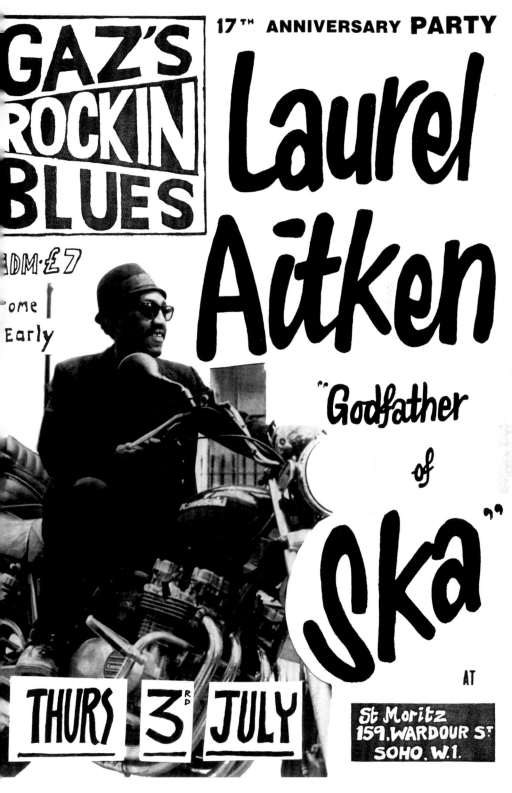

GAZ'S ROCKIN BLUES

St. Moritz
159, Wardour St
Soho, London, W.1.

ADM...£7
or B4 11 £5

THURSDAY
25 SEPT

Doors 10 p.m. — 3.30 A.M.

FEATURING
THE TROJANS '97

"..Earth First!"

THURSDAY 2ND OCT

LIVE...

GAZ'S ROCKIN BLUES

JAKE VEGAS & THE NAKED TRUTH

St. Moritz
159, WARDOUR St
SOHO, W.1.

ADM-£7 come Early
EVERYONE £5 BEFORE 11

9.30 P.M.-3.30 A.M.

GAZ'S ROCKIN BLUES

St. Moritz
159, WARDOUR St
SOHO, W.1.

ADM-£7 come Early
EVERYONE £5 BEFORE 11

THU 16TH OCT

TRAGIC ROUNDABOUT

LIVE

97

GAZ'S ROCKIN BLUES

St. MORITZ CLUB
159, Wardour St.

LONDONS N°1 BLUES DANCE FEATURING LIVE BANDS

ADM-£7
£5 BEFORE 11

FREETOW

I CAN'T WAIT THA

THURSDAY
23RD OCT

GAZ'S ROCKIN BLUES

St. Moritz
159, WARDOUR St
SOHO, W.1.

ADM-£7
EVERYONE
£5 BEFORE 11

LIVE!

THE LIVE INNER Terrestrials!

U.K. Underground

Promoting the New Album...
"FREE THE LAND"

SEPT 11th 97 ☆ ANNA'S BIRTHDAY

GAZ'S ROCKIN BLUES

LONDONS N°1 BLUESDANCE

St. Moritz
159, WARDOUR St
SOHO, W.1.

THURS 4TH SEPT 1997

ADM-£7 EVERYONE £5 BEFORE 11

REBEL LION

Live

GAZ'S ROCKIN BLUES

LONDONS N°1 BLUESDANCE

St. Moritz
159, WARDOUR St
SOHO, W.1.

ADM-£7 come Early
EVERYONE £5 BEFORE 11

THUR 6TH NOV 1997

the Baghdad...es

U.K. UNDERGROUND FESTY CHAMPS!

☆ A LIVE ☆ PERFORMANCE BY THE BAGHPADDIES FROM NEWCASTLE

GAZ'S ROCKIN BLUES

St. MORITZ
159, Wardour St
Soho, London, W.1.

ADM...£7
or B4 11 £5

THURSDAY
18TH SEPT
1997

RUBBE BOOT

featuring

RUNNIN WATER

GAZ'S ROCKIN BLUES

LONDONS № 1 BLUESDANCE

PROUDLY PRESENTING

Sister Asha

Asha

& Guests

LIVE!

St MORITZ
159, Wardour St
Soho, London, W.1

THUR 9TH OCT '97 ♪

♫ ADM·£7 EVERYONE £5 BEFORE 11

FEATURING INNER TERRESTRIALS

GAZ'S ROCKIN BLUES

St Moritz
159 Wardour St
Soho W.1

ALCOHOL
& LIGHT
REFRESHMENTS
PROVIDED

presents

AM'S
19TH BERTHDAY

THURSDAY
11th SEPT'97
10p.m.-4a.m.
LIMITED
EDITION
£5 ENTRANCE
WITH INVITE

R.S.V.P. ANNA MACONOCHIE 0181 249 2924

GAZ'S ROCKIN BLUES

LONDONS № 1 BLUESDANCE

St Moritz
159, WARDOUR St
SOHO. W.1.

ADM·£7 come Early
EVERYONE £5 BEFORE 11

Live

Good Vibes with...

MIND GAP TRILOGY

Solid Soul
- R&B -
Jazz·Funk

on

THURSDAY
7TH AUGUST '97

10PM - 3·30A.M.

GAZ'S ROCKIN BLUES

Nº1 BLUESDANCE

Blackfoot & the Voola
featuring... Rohan "The Man"

St. Moritz, Wardour St. Soho, W.I.

£7 come early
£5 BEFORE 11

10 P.M. - 3.30 A.M.

LIVE!

GOOD ROCKIN'

20 NOV 1997

THURS

THURSDAY 27 NOVEMBER 1997

THE
POETRY BY PATRICK KING

TROJANS

ADM £7   EVERYONE £5 BEFORE 11

LIVE!

St. Moritz, 159, Wardour St Soho. W.I.

GAZ'S ROCKIN BLUES

9.30 P.M. - 3.30 A.M.

GAZ'S ROCKIN BLUES

THURSDAY FEB '98

BOB MARLEY'S BIRTHDAY PARTY

LIVE!

¡T!

INNER TERRESTRIALS

St. Moritz, 159 WARDOUR St SOHO W.I.
10 P.M. 3.30 A.M. ADMISSION £7
£5 BEFORE 11

GAZ'S ROCKIN BLUES

PROUDLY PRESENTS

Live

RUBY THROAT

ST MORITZ
159, Wardour St
Soho, London, W.1.

THURSDAY 15TH JAN 1998

ADM... £7
OR B4 11 £5

Doors 10 PM
until 3.30

GAZ'S ROCKIN BLUES

BARBWIRE LIVE!!

1997

ROCK STEADY BAND FROM THE GROVE !!!

TUFF

Reggae

St. MORITZ CLUB
159, Wardour St.

HU 4 DEC

ADM £7
£5 BEFORE 11

LONDONS Nº1 BLUES DANCE FEATURING LIVE BANDS

GAZ'S ROCKIN BLUES

MEET

Laurel Aitken

AND FREETOWN

XMAS DOLLARAGE PARTY

ADMISSION £8

THURS 18 DEC

LIVE!

THE LAST BLUES OF '97'

"Godfather of Ska"

St Moritz 159, WARDOUR ST SOHO. W.1.

GAZ'S ROCKIN BLUES
LONDONS Nº1 BLUESDANCE

PROUDLY PRESENTS
"STEVE RILEY"
AND THE MAMOU PLAYBOYS
Nº1. CAJUN BAND...
LIVE! FROM U.S.A.

St. Moritz
159, Wardour St.
SOHO. W.1.

ADM...£7
or B4 11 £5

10 P.M. - 3·30 A.M.

THURS 30TH JULY '98

GAZ'S ROCKIN BLUES

St. Moritz club
159, WARDOUR St. W1

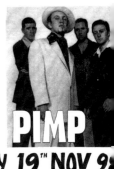

PIMP

THURSDAY 19TH NOV 98

ADM. £7. EVERYONE $5 BEFORE 11 10 - 3·30 A.M.

GAZ'S ROCKIN BLUES
INVITE YOU TO
ST MORITZ
159, Wardour St
Soho, London, W.1.

THURS 30TH APRIL

LAUNCH · PARTY ·
DEBUT ALBUM
CD GAZ 016

PROUDLY PRESENTS
the BAGHDADDIES
LIVE!
ADM £7 EVERYONE $5 BEFORE 11
"LAST TANGO IN BABYLON"

GAZ'S ROCKIN BLUES

St Moritz
159, WARDOUR St
SOHO. W.1.

10 P.M.
ADM £7 come Early
EVERYONE $5 BEFORE 11

PROUDLY PRESENTING
TOP CATS
SKA BAND
LIVE!

18

THURSDAY 7TH MAY 98

GAZ'S ROCKIN BLUES

St. MORITZ blues
159. Wardour St.

Adm. £7. or £5 b4 11

THURSDAY
18TH JUNE 98

"Baba YAGA"

HARD CORE FUNK

GAZ'S ROCKIN BLUES

ST MORITZ
159, Wardour St.
Soho, London, W.1.

ADM...£7
or B4 11 £5

ON THURSDAY
28 MAY '98

FEATURING
THE TROJANS

'Celtic Ska Boys' put Earth First!

GAZ'S ROCKIN BLUES

ST MORITZ
159, Wardour St
Soho, London. W.1.

ADMISSION £9
£7 BEFORE 11

10PM - 3·30AM

THURSDAY 5TH JULY 2007

FEATURING
THE TROJANS
LIVE!
GAZ'S ROCKIN BLUES
27TH ANNIVERSARY

GAZ'S ROCKIN BLUES

ST MORITZ
159, Wardour St
Soho, London. W.1.

ADMISSION £8
£7 BEFORE 11

10PM - 3·30AM

THURSDAY
14TH JUNE 2007

PROUDLY PRESENTING.....
VERY B
LIVE!

CAREFU

FROM LA, USA: COLOMBIA MEXICANA CUM

GAZ'S ROCKIN BLUES

THURS 31ST DECEMBER '98

BY POPULAR DEMAND!

HITMAKER

Alton Ellis

LIVE!

ADM. £12
10 BEFORE 11

GAZ'S ROCKIN' BLUES

NEW YEARS EVE PARTY

STARRING.. THE LEGENDARY JAMAICAN SOUL SINGER.

ALTON ELLIS

SPECIAL!
AT
St. MORITZ CLUB
159, Wardour St.

DOORS
10 P.M.

SOHO
LONDON. W.1.

STEVE HOOKER RUMBLE

GAZ'S ROCKIN BLUES

St. MORITZ CLUB
159, Wardour St.

THURS FEB 18TH

M·£7., £5 BEFORE 11

LIVE!

'99

Carnival of SOULS

LIVE!

APPEARING ON **THURSDAY**
8TH **APRIL**
EMMA, JOSH '99
& TOM'S Birthday

ST MORITZ
159, Wardour St
Soho, London, W.1.

ADM·£7 come Early
EVERYONE £5 BEFORE 11

GAZ'S ROCKIN BLUES

GAZ'S
ROCKIN
BLUES

MORITZ
London, W.1.

RSDAY
MARCH 99

7 come Early
NE £5 BEFORE III

Proudly Presents

DUB-
WISER

LIVE!

♪ ♪

★ FROM OXFORD ★

GAZ'S
ROCKIN
BLUES

LONDONS Nº1 BLUESDANCE

St. Moritz
159, WARDOUR St.
SOHO. W.1.

ADM £7 come Early
EVERYONE £5 BEFORE III

DOORS 10 P.M. CURFEW 3.30 a.m.

THURS 3RD JUNE '99

Checker
PROUDLY PRESENTING
ACE RECORDS
STAX

THE

JAMES
HUNTER
TRIO

LIVE!

GAZ'S
OCKIN
LUES

MORITZ
Wardour St
London, W.1.

£7 £5 BEFORE III

RSDAY 13TH
Y 1999

REBELATION

POWER PACKED REGGAE SKA
~ FROM KINGS LYNN ~

GAZ'S
ROCKIN
BLUES

St. MORITZ CLUB
159, Wardour St.

ADMISSION £7
Come Early!
EVERYONE £5 before 11

THURSDAY
APRIL 15TH 99

DOORS 10 P.M. CURFEW 3.30 a.m.

NUMBER
9

Featuring
PAUL
ANSELL

GAZ'S
OCKIN
LUES

OUR St
or B4 11 £5
ADM...£7

URSDAY
MAR 99

PROUDLY PRESENTS...

I.T.

THE INNER
TERRESTRIALS

GAZ'S
ROCKIN
BLUES

St. Moritz
159, WARDOUR St
SOHO. W.1.

THURSDAY
26TH AUG

ADM £7 come Early
EVERYONE £5 BEFORE III

featuring Linval Golding ♪

THE
Starlite
Junkies

Ska
& Reggae

SPECIAL
'99

GAZ'S
OCKIN
LUES

MORITZ
Wardour St
London, W.1.

1ST
99

3.30 AM

19TH ANNIVERSARY
PARTY

LIVE!

THE TROJANS

GAZ'S
ROCKIN
BLUES

St MORITZ
159 WARDOUR STREET

THURSDAY
15TH JULY
1999

10.30pm-3.30am   Adm £7.00   (Before 11.00pm £5.00)

FEATURING
HEAVY LOADED 60'S SURF BAND

MAGNUM
500

GAZ'S ROCKIN BLUES

LONDONS No.1 BLUESDANCE

ST MORITZ
159, Wardour St
Soho, London, W.1

THE TROJANS

ADM·£7 EVERYONE £5 BEFORE 11

"DESIDERATA"
ON GAZ'S ROCKIN' RECORDS. CD

THURSDAY 4TH NOV '99

10 -

GAZ'S ROCKIN BLUES

PROUDLY PRESENTING FROM J.A.
THE LEGENDARY TROMBONIST...

1999

RICO AND BAND

LAST BLUES OF THE 20TH CENTURY! SPECIAL

ST MORITZ
159, Wardour St
Soho, London, W.1

ADMISSION £8
£7 BEFORE 11

THURS· 30TH DEC

9.30 A.M-3.30 P.M.

GAZ'S ROCKIN BLUES

LIVE

LOR

INNOCENT

AT St. Moritz
159, Wardour St
Soho, W.1

ADM·£7
£5 BEFORE 11

THURS 28TH OCT '99

SKA

FROM GERMA

GAZ'S ROCKIN BLUES

PROUDLY PRESENTING

THE **TOP CATS**

AUTHENTIC SKA BAND

TOP 18 REGGAE

ST MORITZ
159, Wardour St
Soho, London, W.1.

ADM·£7 come early
EVERYONE £5 BEFORE 11

THURS 11TH NOV '99

GAZ'S ROCKIN BLUES

The **BRIGHTO**

AGITATOR

10 - PIECE

SKA

10 - 3·30 A.M.

ST MORITZ
159, Wardour St
Soho, London, W.1.

THURS 24TH FEB 2000

ADM·£7 £5 BEFORE 11

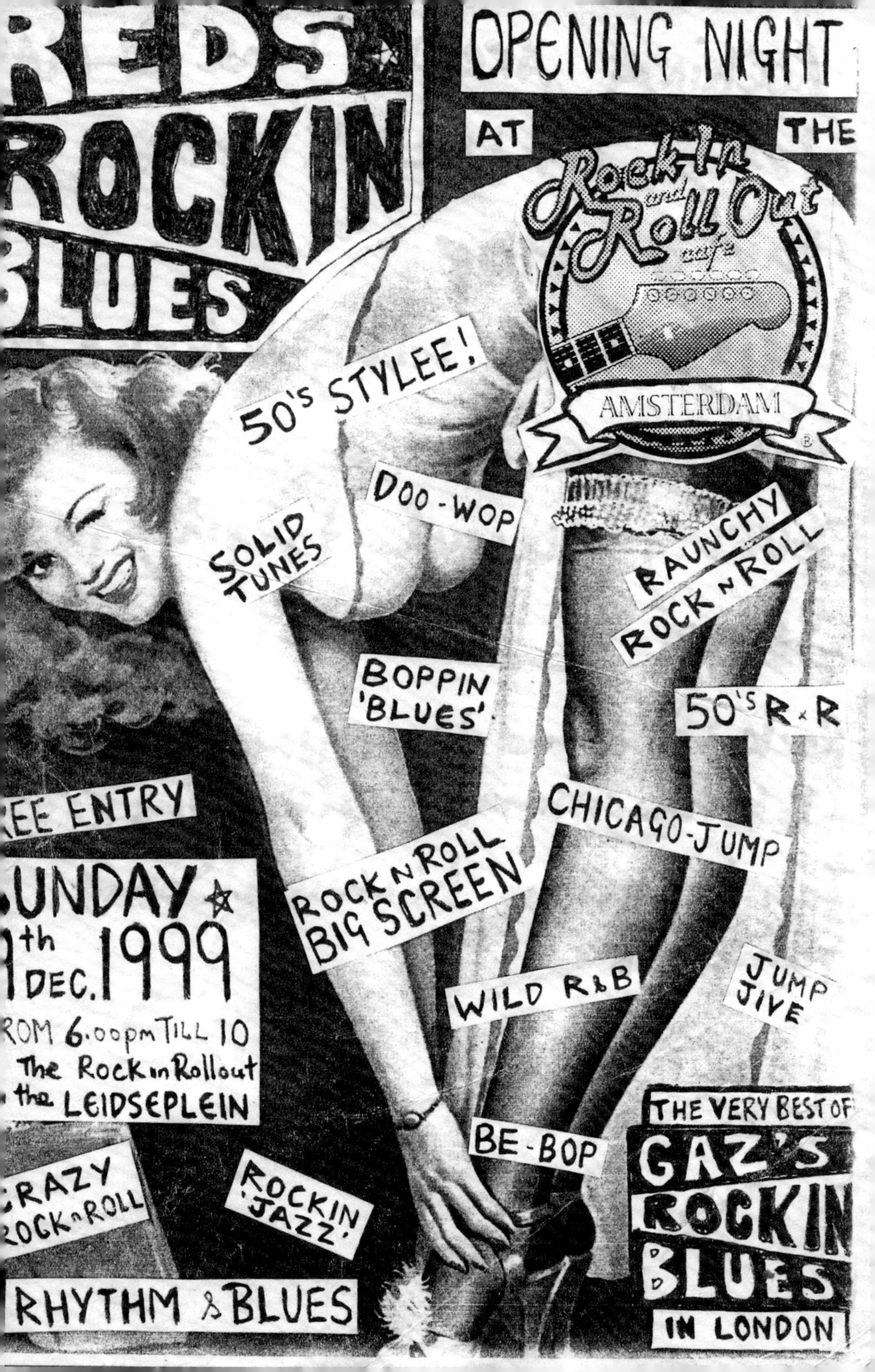

REDS ROCKIN BLUES

OPENING NIGHT

AT THE

Rock In and Roll Out café

AMSTERDAM

50's STYLEE!

SOLID TUNES

DOO-WOP

RAUNCHY ROCK n ROLL

BOPPIN 'BLUES'

50's R x R

CHICAGO-JUMP

ROCK n ROLL BIG SCREEN

FREE ENTRY

SUNDAY 19th DEC. 1999
FROM 6.00pm TILL 10
The Rock in Rollout
the LEIDSEPLEIN

WILD R&B

JUMP JIVE

BE-BOP

THE VERY BEST OF GAZ'S ROCKIN BLUES IN LONDON

CRAZY ROCK n ROLL

ROCKIN 'JAZZ'

RHYTHM & BLUES

GAZ'S ROCKIN BLUES

St Moritz
159, WARDOUR St
SOHO. W.1.

ADM...£7
OR B4 11 £5

THURSDAY
3RD FEB
2000

TOM LaVelle & the Houserockers

Jerry Lee Lewis style Rock 'n' Roll from U.S.A.

GAZ'S ROCKIN BLUES

LONDONS Nº 1 BLUESDANCE

ST MORITZ
159, Wardour St
Soho, London, W.1.

ADM·£7 come Early
EVERYONE £5 BEFORE 11

THURS 10TH
FEB 2000

Highway 5

BLUES COMBO

GAZ'S ROCKIN BLUES

THURS 6TH JAN

ST MORITZ
159, Wardour St
Soho, London, W.1.

— PROUDLY PRESENTS —

SKA -GAL & THE HaNDS OF RA

ADM·£7 £5 BEFORE 11

2000

joe West.

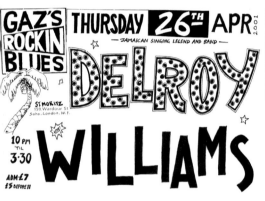

GAZ'S ROCKIN BLUES

PRESENTS GYPSY ROOTS GROUP LIVE

MUKKA

ST MORITZ
159, Wardour St
Soho, London, W.1.

ADM: £7
£5 BEFORE 11

THURS 13th
JULY '00

GAZ'S ROCKIN BLUES

ST MORITZ
159, Wardour St
Soho, London, W.1.

THURSDAY
30 MARCH
2000

ROBOT IN DISGUISE

All-Girl Soupa Group

GAZ'S ROCKIN BLUES

ADY 'GUITAR' BELL BLUES TRIO

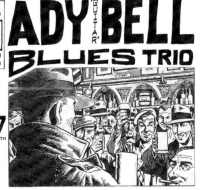

ST MORITZ
159, Wardour St.

THURSDAY
APRIL 27th
2000

ADM £7 come Early
EVERYONE £5 BEFORE 11

GAZ'S ROCKIN BLUES

ST MORITZ
159, Wardour St
Soho, London, W.1.

LIVE!

THUR 13th
APRIL 2000

ADM. £7. or £5 B411

PROPOGANDA AND P.A.I.N INFORMATION

GAZ'S ROCKIN BLUES

LIVE!

THURS
1st
JUNE
2000

ST MORITZ
159, Wardour St
Soho, London, W.1.

10 PM — 3.30 AM
"DESIDERATA TOUR"

ADM· £7
EVERYONE £5 BEFORE 11

THE TROJANS

GAZ'S ROCKIN BLUES

ST MORITZ
159, Wardour St
Soho, London, W.1.

ADM £7 come Early
EVERYONE £5 BEFORE 11

THURSDAY
12 OCT
2000

Proudly presents...The

HULLABALUES

AUTHENTIC 1950's
R&B

LIVE!

GAZ'S ROCKIN BLUES

ST MORITZ
159, Wardour St
Soho, London, W.1.

ADM £7 come Early
EVERYONE £5 BEFORE 11

THURS
3rd AUGUST
2000

SHOT IN THE DARK

SKA & REGGAE

GAZ'S ROCKIN BLUES

SKA & Reggae
KINGSIZE
From... Leicester.

ST MORITZ
159, Wardour St
Soho, London, W.1.

ADM·£7
£5 BEFORE 11

THURSDAY 17TH AUG

AZ'S ROCKIN LUES
NS N°1 BLUESDANCE

ST MORITZ
oho, London, W.1.

THURSDAY
TH AUG
2000
£7 £5 BEFORE 11

TRANSFORMER
FEATURING SWITZERLANDS NUMBER 1 REGGAE BAND

GAZ'S ROCKIN BLUES

PRESENTS **THE**

ST MORITZ
159, Wardour St
Soho, London, W.1.

ADM·£7
£5 BEFORE 11

THURS 5TH OCT '00

HERBERT SPLIFFINGTON
ALLSTARS STARRING **SATCH**

AZ'S ROCKIN LUES

ST MORITZ
159, Wardour St
oho, London, W.1.

ADM...£7
or B4 11 £5

URS 28TH SEPT '00

TOO HOT

GAZ'S ROCKIN BLUES
LONDONS N°1 BLUESDANCE

ST MORITZ
159, Wardour St
Soho, London, W.1.

ADMISSION £7
Come Early!
EVERYONE £5 BEFORE 11

THURS 10TH MAY 2001

PROUDLY PRESENTS ...

ZION TRAIN

GAZ'S ROCKIN BLUES

THURSDAY 20 DECEMBER

St. Moritz. 159, Wardour St Soho. W.1.

STARRING

ROY SHIRLEY

FROM JAMAICA

ROCKSTEADY

LIVE!

2001

ADM·£8. Come Early!
EVERYONE £6 BEFORE 11

GAZ'S ROCKIN BLUES

THE BAD TEMPERED CYRILS

St MORITZ
159, Wardour St
Soho, London, W.1.

THURS.

3RD

JAN

2002

Live Punk

ADM·**£7** come Early
EVERYONE **£5** BEFORE 11

GAZ'S ROCKIN BLUES

St. MORITZ CLUB
159, WARDOUR St. W.1

ADM. £7, EVERYONE **£5** BEFORE 11

STARRING...

10-3·30 AM

F 'RIALTO'
+
'KINKY MACHINE'

SUPPORTED BY

MIAMI RED
(Bluesman Guitarist)

LOUIS ELIOT

THURS 28TH FEB 2002

GAZ'S ROCKIN BLUES

AT **ST MORITZ** ADM. **£7**
159, Wardour St £5
Soho, London, W.1. BEFORE 11 P.M.

THURSDAY
30th MAY '02

STARRING WITH

LITTLE
GEORGE SUEREF
& The Blue Stars

GAZ'S ROCKIN BLUES

ST MORITZ
159, Wardour St
Soho. London. W.1.

ADM. £7 come Early
EVERYONE £5 BEFORE 11

THURSDAY
14th NOV
2002

GAZ'S ROCKIN BLUES

St Moritz
159, WARDOUR ST
SOHO. W.1.

ADM·£7 come Early
EVERYONE £5 BEFORE 11

THURSDAY

FROM OUT OF THE FUTURE..HE APP
COME TO PA
by way
ADMISSION
£5
FEATURED DJ'S
Count Cassavubu
ROCK STEADY EDDIE

CLUB SKA

10th Anniversary Live

Special Guest DJ GAZ MAYALL MO

CLUB SKA ALL STA

'98.5.16 (SAT)

start 9:00 at WIRE

¥3,000-[2DRINK]

KING NABE * PRINCE MATSUOKA *
BAMBOO TAKEI * RAS TARO *
Dr.JHARA * BIG TANAKA *
FLOWER HANADA * GUN SEKI *

問い合わせ * CLUB WIRE * B1 HANAZONO BLDG. 5-17-6 SHINJUKU ☎ 03(3207

[SKA EXPPLOSION'98] SKATALITES   start 1:30

CLUB SKA

THE TROJANS
SKA FLAMES at 日比谷野外音楽

TOKYO SKAPARADISE ORCHESTRA
+ MORE   前売: 指定¥6,000 / 自由¥

'98.5.17 (SUN)

問い合わせ * SMASH * ☎03(3444)6751

GAZ'S ROCKIN BLUES

SPECIAL TOP SKA DJ of the World

GAZ MAYALL

(from LONDON)
AND DJs
KOHZU
(Determinations)
DRU-WEED
TOP SKA YODA

5 18 MON FEE2000

METRO
075 752 4765

GAZ'S ROCKIN BLUES

ST MORITZ
159, Wardour St
Soho, London, W.1.

THURSDAY 25TH
MAY 2000

ADM·£7 come Early
EVERYONE £5 BEFORE 11

PROUDLY PRES

GAZ'S ROCKIN BLUES

~ XMAS PARTY ~

LIVE SKA/ROCK STEADY FROM THE U.S.A.
IN LONDON FOR ONE NIGHT ONLY......

ERIC BLOWTORCH & The INFLAMMABLES

ST MORITZ
159, Wardour St
Soho, London, W.1.

ADM · £8.

Come Early!

EVERYONE

£6 BEFORE 11

☆

THURS

19

DEC

2002

☆

10 - 3·30 AM

浪花ロッキンブルース

2003.2.11.
National Foundation Day
17:00-23:00@CLUB DAWN
adv 2,500yen/door 3,000yen

GAZ'S ROCKIN BLUES

GAZ MAYALL
(THE TROJANS/Gaz's Rockin' Blues)

ru-weed (Drum&Bass Records)

KUMURA (カリエンテレコード)

UCCHIE (Small Axe Records)

HIN THE 88 (Drum&Bass Records)

ONE (OSAKA SKANKIN' NIGHT)

N&DOI&BON (Let's Moon STOMP!)

HE MICETEETH ALL STARS

(CAFE MEETING)

EN (SKA BAR)

MAYALL

昨年のフジロックフェスティバルにDJとして来日した
ギャズメイオールはSKA、R&B、BLUESのビンテージ
レコードコレクターであり、業界随一のパフォーマンスDJ
として世界的に広く知られる。また、1980年代後半〜
1990年代初頭にかけ一大ムーブメントを起こした
UK SKA BAND『THE TROJANS』のリーダーである
彼は、自らオーガナイズするDJイベント『Gaz's Rockin'
s』を日本でも数回開催しており、大盛況をおさめている。
はここ大阪CLUB DAWN にて浪花を代表するビンテージSKA DJ陣とコラボ
し、『浪花ロッキンブルース』として、全SKAファン必見必聴のPARTYが開催される。

presented by

PROJECT

tion by TAMAKI TSUGAWA,photograph by MASAYUKI KUDO,design by ATSUSHI TAKASAKI ☺

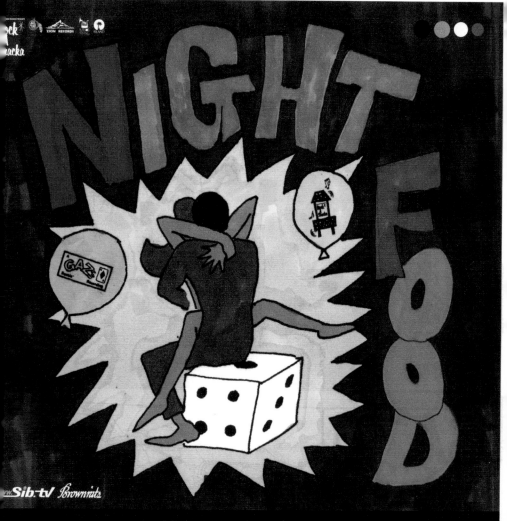

DRUM & BASS RECORDS PRESENTS

NIGHT FOOD SPECIAL

GUEST DJ:
GAZ MAYALL

DJ:
DRUWEED (DRUM & BASS RECORDS), SHIN (DETERMINATIONS)
MASAKI MORI (EGO-WRAPPIN'), TOMMY (DRUM & BASS RECORDS)
TERA-SUN (ISLAND)

OYAMA FAI

20 (SUN) 22:00 OPEN/START
DV. 3,000YEN (1 D) / DOOR. 3,500YEN (1 D)
b. AOYAMA FAI 03. 3486. 4910

SKA
ROCK STEADY
REGGAE
CALYPSO
JAZZ
R&B
BAAAD, HOOOT BUT SWEETEST MUZIK
FROM JAMAICA

なんば MACAO

8/1 (FRI) 22:00 OPEN/START
ADV. 3,000YEN (1 D) / DOOR. 3,500YEN (1 D)
info. DRUM & BASS RECORDS 06. 6211. 1044

Hatihonkan ビルB1/2F
AOYAMA FAI

SPIRAL

富士銀行 　紀ノ国屋 　青山通

表参道

青山学院

骨董通

千日前通

御堂筋　難波本通

難波　なんば　オリエンタルホテル

高島屋　南海通　なんばグランド花月

日本橋

堺筋

味園ビルB1
MACAO

なんばプラザホテル

GAZ'S ROCKIN BLUES
LONDONS Nº 1 BLUESDANCE

St Moritz
159, WARDOUR ST
SOHO, W.1.

MUTTLY'S DASTARDLY SKAM

THURS **3rd OCT**

ADM·£7
£5 BEFORE 11

GAZ'S ROCKIN BLUES

St MORITZ
159, Wardour St
Soho, London, W.1.

ADM·£7 ... £5 BEFORE 11

THURSDAY

16th JAN 2003

ronnie King
LIVE TONIGHT

& HIS "C" MEN

slick rock 'n' roll sleaze

THURSDAY — 1 AUGUST — 2002

DENNIS ALCAPONE

ADMISSION £8 £7 BEFORE 11

GAZ'S ROCKIN BLUES

ST MORITZ
159, Wardour St
Soho, London. W.1.

ADM £7 . , . £5 BEFORE 11

RONNIE KING

& his "C" men

LIVE!

THURSDAY 15TH AUG 2002

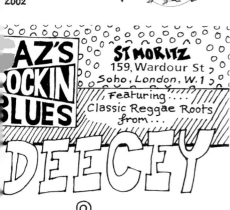

GAZ'S ROCKIN BLUES

ST MORITZ
9, Wardour St
, London, W.1.
7   £5 BEFORE 11

THURSDAY
SEPT
2002

SKA REVUE FROM BRIGHTON

YE-Wiles

LIVE!

GAZ'S ROCKIN BLUES

LONDONS N°1 BLUESDANCE

St Moritz
159, WARDOUR ST
SOHO. W.1.

ADM £7
£5 BEFORE 11

THURSDAY 27TH FEB '03

KING SNAKES

LIVE!

ROCK 'N' ROLL

GAZ'S ROCKIN BLUES

ST MORITZ
159, Wardour St
Soho, London, W.1

Featuring...
Classic Reggae Roots
from...

DEECEY

& the FAMILY PACT

THURSDAY
2 AUG '02
ADMISSION £7
Come Early!
EVERYONE £5 BEFORE 11

GAZ'S ROCKIN BLUES

LONDONS N°1 BLUESDANCE

ST MORITZ
159, Wardour St
Soho, London, W.1.

ADM £7 ... £5 BEFORE 11

THURSDAY
22ND MAY 2003

PROUDLY PRESENTS
SWEDISH PUNK BAND

THE DANDELIONS

10 P.M-3.30AM

GAZ'S ROCKIN BLUES

ST MORITZ
159, Wardour St
Soho, London, W.1.

ADM £7 come Early
EVERYONE £5 before 11

THURSDAY
5TH DEC '2

10 P.M-3.30AM

SMERINS ANTI-SOCIAL CLUB

LIVE!   LIVE!

latindubfunkflamencorockexperience

GAZ'S ROCKIN BLUES

PROUDLY PRESENT

LUDDY SAMMS —AND THE— SOUL DELIVERERS

(ELINORS BIRTHDAY PARTY)

St MORITZ 159 WARDOUR St W1

ADM £7 BEFORE 11

10 PM - THURSDAY - 3.30 AM

30th JAN

2003

GAZ'S ROCKIN BLUES

From Japan...

Little Tempo

ADM £7 £5 BEFORE 11

at St. Moritz 159. Wardour St ~ Soho. W.1

Top Reggae Act...

THURSDAY 26th JUN '03

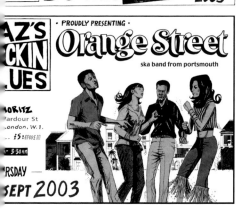

GAZ'S ROCKIN BLUES

· PROUDLY PRESENTING ·

Orange Street

ska band from portsmouth

St MORITZ Wardour St London. W.1. £5 BEFORE 10 - 3.30am

THURSDAY

SEPT 2003

GAZ'S ROCKIN BLUES

LONDONS No 1 BLUESDANCE

PROUDLY PRESENTS

MAZAIKA

St. Moritz 159. WARDOUR St SOHO. W.1

ADM £7 come Early EVERYONE £5 BEFORE 11

DOORS 10 P.M. CURFEW 3.30am

RUSSIAN GYPSYS

THURS 2nd OCTOBER '03

GAZ'S ROCKIN BLUES

THE VINCENTS

St Moritz, WARDOUR St SOHO. W.1.

THURSDAY

14TH

AUGUST '03

ADM £7 come Early EVERYONE £5 BEFORE 11

THURS 12th JUN '03

LIVE!

LADY & The Tramps

GAZ'S ROCKIN BLUES

ADM £7 come Early EVERYONE £5 BEFORE 11

Sexy, Slick 'n' sleazy 40's & 50's R&B

St MORITZ 159. Wardour St Soho. London. W.1

GAZ'S ROCKIN BLUES

RUMBLESTRIP

HEARTBREAK SNAKES

ADMISSION £7 Come Early! EVERYONE £5 BEFORE 11

DOUBLE FEATURE

SPECIAL THURS 7TH AUG 2003

LONDONS No 1 BLUES DANCE TURING LIVE BANDS

GAZ & THE ROCKIN BLUES GANG

GAZ'S ROCKIN BLUES

St MORITZ 159 Wardour St Soho. London. W.1

ADM £7 come Early EVERYONE £5 BEFORE 11

THURSDAY 9TH OCT 2003

The Slammers

LIVE!

punk Rock & Roll

YOU DIDN'T HAVE TO KILL HIM!

HE DESERVED IT! HE KILLED TWO OF MY BOYS!

10 P.M. - 3.30 AM

GAZ'S ROCKIN BLUES

LONDON'S Nº 1 BLUESDANCE

PROUDLY PRESENTING.....

THE ZEN HUSSIES LIVE!

AT ST MORITZ ADM. £7
159, Wardour St £5
Soho, London, W.1. BEFORE 11 P.M.

10 P.M - 3:30 A.M

— THURSDAY —

9TH SEPT 2004 Swing-ska Rockin' Revue

GAZ'S ROCKIN BLUES

ST MORITZ
159, Wardour St
Soho, London, W.1.

THURS 5TH AUGUST 2004

MAROON TOWN

ADMISSION £7 EVERYONE £5 BEFORE 11 10 P.M - 3:30 A.M

GAZ'S ROCKIN BLUES

LONDON'S Nº 1 BLUESDANCE

★ ST MORITZ
159 Wardour Street

ADM £7... £5 BEFORE 11

10 P.M - 3:30 A.M

THURSDAY 16TH DECEMBER 2004

HIPBONE SLIM
AND THE KNEE-TREMBLERS LIVE!

GAZ'S ROCKIN BLUES

ST MORITZ
159, Wardour St
Soho, London, W.1.

ADM £7... £5 BEFORE 11

— THURSDAY —

FEB 10 2005

son of dav

dynamic blues har
wizard rave mac

GAZ'S ROCKIN BLUES

LONDON'S Nº 1 BLUESDANCE

ST MORITZ
159, Wardour St
Soho, London, W.1.

ADM £7... £5 BEFORE 11

10 P.M - 3:30 A.M

THURSDAY 14TH APRIL 2005

RED'S BIRTHDAY PARTY
PROUDLY PRESENTING
ROCKABILLY TRIO appearing Live!

The NIGHT SHAKERS

GAZ'S ROCKIN BLUES

ST MORITZ
159, Wardour St
Soho, London, W.1.

ADM £7... £5 BEFORE 11

10 P.M - 3:30 A.M

THURSDAY 4TH NOV 04

JOIN IN THE GOOD VIBRATION
TO ROCK THE NATION,
LISTEN TO THE SOUNDS OF THE...

8 PIECE BAND

No.1 **STATIO**

Featuring the legendary tru
Eddie 'Tan Tan'

ORIGIN
SK
ROCKST
REGG
60s 70
STYL

LIV

GAZ'S ROCKIN BLUES

★ ST MORITZ
159 Wardour Street

ADM £7... £5 BEFORE 11

10 P.M - 3:30 A.M

THURSDAY OCTOBER 28 2004

PROUDLY PRESENTING.....

CIRCUS SOUNDS TO WAKE THE DEAD
HALLOWEEN MUSIC FROM SWITZERLAND

THE DEAD BROTHERS LIVE!

GAZ'S ROCKIN BLUES

PRESENTS

AT
ST MORITZ
159, Wardour St
Soho, London, W.1.

THE **AMPHETA MEANIES**

THURS MAY

LIVE: BAD ASS SC
FROM

10 P.M - 3:30 A.M ADM £7... £5 BEFORE 11

PROUDLY PRESENTING.....

GAZ'S ROCKIN BLUES

the Cordwood Draggers

rockabilly trio

LIVE!

ST MORITZ
159, Wardour St
Soho, London, W.1.

10 P.M - 3:30 A.M

ADM £7... £5 BEFORE 11

THURSDAY
PRIL 1 2004

AZ'S ROCKIN BLUES

moritz. 159, Wardour St Soho. W.1.

LIVE!

• PROUDLY PRESENTING •

FROM JAMAICA

ROY SHIRLEY

ROCKSTEADY

PRE-RELEASE LAUNCH PARTY OF TOP SKA
COMPILED BY GAZ MAYALL ON TROJAN RECORDS

THURSDAY
18 MARCH 2004

ADM £8. Come Early!
EVERYONE £6 BEFORE 11

3·30 A.M.

GAZ'S ROCKIN BLUES

FEATURING ...

THE VELOURS

10 P.M - 3:30 A.M

LIVE!

THURS 25 MARCH 2004

ADM £7... £5 BEFORE 11

★ ST MORITZ
159 Wardour Street

R&B

GAZ'S ROCKIN BLUES

ST MORITZ
159, Wardour St
Soho, London, W.1.

ADM·£7 come Early
EVERYONE £5 BEFORE 11

THURSDAY
6TH MAY 2004

PROUDLY PRESENTING...

LIVE!

Vincent Vincent AND THE VILLAINS

10 P.M - 3:30 A.M

GAZ'S ROCKIN BLUES

10 P.M - 3:

D.J. the legendar

Duke Vin

ST MORITZ
159, Wardour St
Soho, London, W.1.

THUR 13 MAY 2004

ADMISSION
Come Ear
EVERYONE £5 BE

GAZ'S ROCKIN BLUES
FEATURING... The BiG
SKA!
LIVE!
ST MORITZ
59, Wardour St
Soho, London. W.1.
ADMISSION £7 Come Early!
EVERYONE £5 BEFORE 11
THURSDAY
MAY 2004

GAZ'S ROCKIN BLUES
LONDONS No 1 BLUESDANCE
St. Moritz
159, WARDOUR ST
SOHO. W.1.
ADM £7 come Early
EVERYONE £5 BEFORE 11
DOORS 10 P.M. CURFEW 3.30 A.M.
THURSDAY
10TH JUNE 2004
PROUDLY PRESENTING
STAX
THE JAMES HUNTER TRIO
LIVE!
TOP CLASS 50's 60's R&B

GAZ'S ROCKIN BLUES
No 1 BLUESDANCE
ST MORITZ
9, Wardour St
Soho, London. W.1.
ADM £7 come Early
EVERYONE £5 BEFORE 11
THURSDAY
APRIL 2004
BABYHEAD
10 Piece SKA Band From Bristol
LIVE!

GAZ'S ROCKIN BLUES
PROUDLY PRESENTING....
HEAVY LOADED 60'S SURF BAND
MAGNUM 500
★ST MORITZ
159 Wardour Street
ADM £7 come Early
EVERYONE £5 BEFORE 11
LIVE!
THURSDAY
17 JUNE 2004
10PM - 3.30AM

GAZ'S ROCKIN BLUES
No 1 BLUESDANCE
MORITZ
Wardour Street
ADMISSION £7
Come Early!
THURSDAY
JULY 2004
10 - 3.30AM
PROUDLY PRESENTING....
Rockin' Variety with
THE **HOUSEROCKERS**
LIVE!
Rock and Roll Youths 'Wild'
David M. Nichol
destruction and disorder followed
HOUSEROCKERS tour thru Germany

GAZ'S ROCKIN BLUES
LONDONS No 1 BLUESDANCE
★ST MORITZ
159 Wardour Street
ADM £7 come Early
EVERYONE £5 BEFORE 11
THURSDAY
29TH JULY 2004
PROUDLY PRESENTING IRELANDS GREATEST BLUES GUITARIST
JIM CARLISE & his Jumpin Jacks
plus
the **contra-band**
LIVE!
10PM - 3.30AM

GAZ'S ROCKIN BLUES
LONS No 1 BLUESDANCE
ST MORITZ
59, Wardour St
Soho, London. W.1.
THURSDAY
JAN 2005
10PM - 3.30AM
· PROUDLY PRESENTING ·
LIVE!
FASTLANE RODGELATOR

GAZ'S ROCKIN BLUES
LONDONS No 1 BLUESDANCE
ST MORITZ
159, Wardour St
Soho. London. W.1.
10PM - 3.30AM
ADM £7... £5 BEFORE 11
THURSDAY
MAR 3 2005
PROUDLY PRESENTING....
CHICKEN SHED ZEPPELIN
LIVE!
FIDDLETHRASHIN' YEEHARHOLLERIN'
OLE-TIME STRING BAND

GAZ'S ROCKIN BLUES

FEATURING...
FROM LA, USA... TOP SKA...SKINHEAD REGGAE

PLUS: REBEL SKA BAND
FROM LITHUANIA

THE AGGROLITES DR. GREEN

ST MORITZ
159, Wardour St
Soho, London, W.1.

ADM·£7 come Early
EVERYONE £5 BEFORE 11

10 P.M - 3:30 A.M

HURSDAY
1 APRIL 05

GAZ'S ROCKIN BLUES

· PROUDLY PRESENTING ·
HIGH TOWN CROWS   LIVE!

MORITZ
ardour Street
P.M - 3:30A.M
7... £5 BEFORE 11

URSDAY
TH MARCH
2005

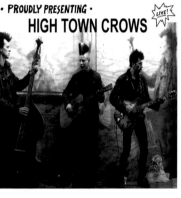

GAZ'S ROCKIN BLUES

PROUDLY PRESENTING.....
The Urban Voodoo Machine
BOURBON SOAKED GYPSY BLUES BOP'N'STROLL   LIVE!

S N° 1 BLUESDANCE
MORITZ
ardour Street
... £5 BEFORE 11
P.M - 3:30A.M

URSDAY
JUNE
005

GAZ'S ROCKIN BLUES

AT ST MORITZ   ADM. £7
159, Wardour St £5
Soho, London, W.1. BEFORE 11 P.M.

THURS 16TH JUNE
2005

PROUDLY PRESENTING.....

The Magic Number

GYPSY, JAZZ, SWING
FROM BRIGHTON....   LIVE!

10 P.M - 3:30 A.M

GAZ'S ROCKIN BLUES

LONDONS Nº 1 BLUESDANCE

ST MORITZ

159, Wardour St
Soho, London, W.1.

**ADMISSION £8
£7 BEFORE 11**

10 P.M - 3:30 A.M

THURSDAY

31ˢᵀ

MARCH 2005

• **PROUDLY PRESENTING**

CHRIS FARLOWE

BACKED BY PAUL ANSELL'S THUNDERBIRDS

LIVE!

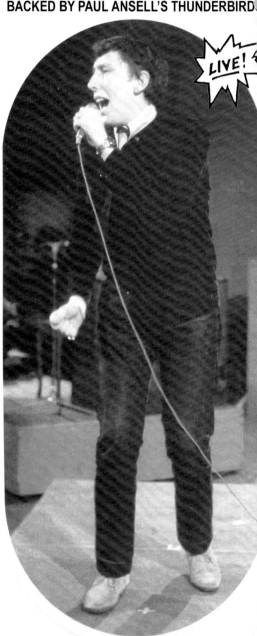

GAZ'S ROCKIN BLUES

• PROUDLY PRESENTING •

ALCO MONKEY SKA FROM

LIVE!

7 SECONDS OF LOVE

ST MORITZ

59, Wardour St
oho, London, W.1.

10 P.M - 3:30 A.M

ADMISSION £7
Come Early!
EVERYONE £5 BEFORE 11

HURSDAY

12TH

MAY

2005

PROUDLY PRESENTING.....

GAZ'S ROCKIN BLUES

the Cordwood Draggers

rockabilly tri

LIVE!

ST MORITZ
159, Wardour St
Soho, London, W.1.

10 P.M - 3:30 A.M

ADM·£7... £5 BEFORE 11

THURSDAY
MAR 17 2005

GAZ'S ROCKIN BLUES

PROUDLY PRESENTING : HITMAKER FROM JAMAICA ..

DAVE
"DOUBLE BARREL"-"MONKEY SPANNER"
BARKER

ST MORITZ
159, Wardour St
Soho, London, W.1.

ADMISSION £8
£7 BEFoRE 11

10 P.M - 3:30 A.M

THURSDAY
JULY 21 2005

♫ with ♫
★ FREETOWN
gaz's rockin blues 25th anniversary party spec

GAZ'S ROCKIN BLUES

ST MORITZ
159, Wardour St
Soho. London. W.1.

ADMISSION £8
£7 BEFORE 11

THURSDAY
4TH JULY
2005
P.M- 3:30 A.M

PROUDLY PRESENTING.....

From St. Louis, Mo, USA. R&B, SOUL Sensation.

Jimmy Thomas

With LITTLE GEORGE SUEREF & The Blue Stars

LIVE!

gaz's rockin' blues 25th anniversary party special

GAZ'S ROCKIN BLUES

ST MORITZ
59, Wardour St
ho, London, W.1.

MISSION £8 · £7 BEFORE 11

THURSDAY
TH JULY
2005

PROUDLY PRESENTING.....

...BRIXTON SKA

LIVE!

TOP CATS

featuring
Special guest appearance of
Benny Billy (Ska Cubano)

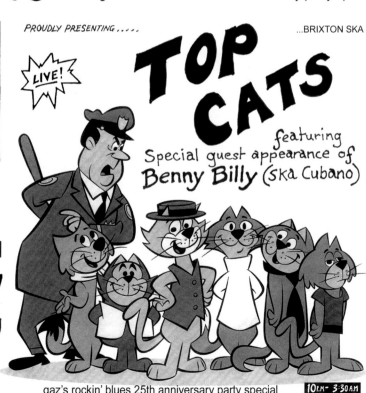

gaz's rockin' blues 25th anniversary party special

10 P.M- 3:30 A.M

GAZ'S ROCKIN BLUES
LONDONS Nº 1 BLUESDANCE

James Hunter
and his band

St Moritz
159, WARDOUR ST
SOHO. W.1.

LIVE!

ADM·£7 come Early

EVERYONE £5 BEFORE 11

DOORS 10 P.M. CURFEW 3·30 A.M.

— THURSDAY —

4TH AUGUST 2005

gaz's rockin' blues 25th anniversary party sp

GAZ'S ROCKIN BLUES

PROUDLY PRESENTING: HITMAKER FROM JAMAICA

Winston
"Mr Fix It"
Francis

with

★★★ INTENSIFIED ★★★

ST MORITZ
159, Wardour St
Soho, London, W.1.

ADMISSION £8
£7 BEFoRE 11

10 P.M - 3:30 A.M

THURSDAY
18TH AUGUST
2005

gaz's rockin blues 25th anniversary party spec

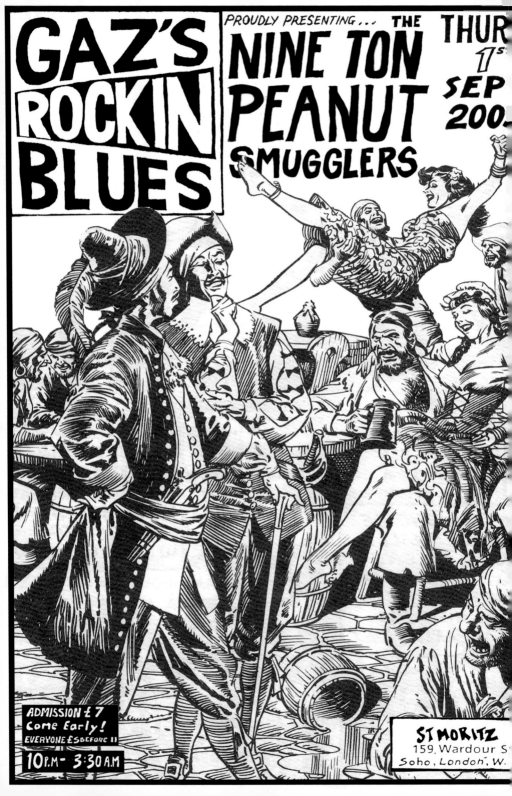

GAZ'S ROCKIN BLUES

· PROUDLY PRESENTING ·

THE BOLLOCK

BROTHERS

★ AT ST MORITZ

159 Wardour Street

ADMISSION £8
Come Early!
EVERYONE £6 BEFORE 11

THURSDAY

SEPTEMBER

13TH 2007

10 P.M - 3:30

GAZ'S ROCKIN BLUES

LONDONS Nº 1 BLUESDANCE

AT ST MORITZ ADM. £7
159, Wardour St £5
Soho, London, W. 1. BEFORE 11 P.M.

10 P.M - 3:30 A.M

THURSDAY 13
APRIL 2006

LIVE!

GOLDMASTER ALLSTARS

10 PIECE ROOTS, REGGAE & AUTHENTIC SI

GAZ'S ROCKIN BLUES

★ ST MORITZ

159 Wardour Street

ADMISSION £7
Come Early!
EVERYONE £5 BEFORE 11

10 P.M - 3:30 A.M

THURSDAY
25 MAY 2006

DOMINO BON█S

FROM MANCHESTER
MONICA, WINKER, \

GAZ'S ROCKIN BLUES

NDONS №1 BLUESDANCE

PROUDLY PRESENTING.....

SONNY WEST AND THE CONGO FAITH HEALERS

LIVE!

AT *ST MORITZ*
159, Wardour St
Soho, London, W.1.

ADM. £8
£6
BEFORE 11 P.M.

10 P.M - 3:30 A.M

THURS 3RD AUGUST 2006

GAZ'S ROCKIN BLUES

PROUDLY PRESENTING...

THE SELECTER

LIVE!

ST MORITZ
59 Wardour Street

ADM. £10.

Come Early £8 BEFORE 11

THUR 31ST AUGUST 06

10 P.M - 3:30 A.M

CELEBRATING 50 YEARS OF BRITISH ROCK&ROLL, SKIFFLE, BLUES AND R&B

GAZ'S ROCKIN BLUES

THE BLOWEEVILS

LONDONS Nº 1 BLUESDA

ST MORITZ
159, Wardour St
Soho, London, W.1.

ADM £8... £6 BEFORE 11

THURSDAY
27TH JULY
2006

LIVE!

10PM - 3:30AM

PROUDLY PRESENTING....

GAZ'S ROCKIN BLUES

★ST MORITZ
159 Wardour Street
ADMISSION £8 • £6 BEFORE 11

10PM - 3:30AM

THURSDAY
29TH JUNE
2006

THE RACKETEER
Ska band from Ports

GAZ'S ROCKIN BLUES

PROUDLY PRESENTING....

THE SKAMONICS

ST MORITZ
159, Wardour St
Soho, London, W.1.

10PM - 3:30AM

ADM £7... £5 BEFORE 11

THURSDAY
1ST JUNE 06

JAZZ MEETS SKA LONDON STYLE

GAZ'S ROCKIN BLUES

PROUDLY PRESENTING....

BOY LE MONT
VINTAGE SKA, ROCK STEADY
AND OTHER EXCELLENT TUNES

LIVE!

AT ST MORITZ ADM. £7
159, Wardour St £5
Soho, London, W.1. BEFORE 11 PM.

THURSDAY
12TH OCTOBER 2006

10P

GAZ'S ROCKIN BLUES

- PROUDLY PRESENTING -
ON THURS 2ND
NOVEMBER 2006
from japan: all-girl garage
punk group

ST MORITZ
159, Wardour St
Soho, London.
W.1.

SPOOKEY!

LIVE!

+ Brighton ska band!
MEE-OW
MEE-OW!

ADMISSION £7
Come Early!
EVERYONE £5 BEFORE 11

10P.M - 3:30AM

GAZ'S ROCKIN BLUES

PROUDLY PRESENTING....

SMASHIN TIME
LIVE!
THURSDAY 16T
NOVEMBER
200

Care to dance?

ADMISSION £7
Come Early!
EVERYONE £5 BEFORE 11

ST MORITZ
159, Wardour St
Soho, London, W.1.

10P.M - 3

GAZ'S ROCKIN BLUES

LONDONS Nº 1 BLUESDANCE

PROUDLY PRESENTS

ROLLO MARKEE
& THE TAILSHAKERS

AT *ST MORITZ* ADM. £7
159, Wardour St £5
Soho, London, W.1. BEFORE 11 P.M.

THURSDAY
OCTOBER
19ᵀᴴ 2006

LIVE!

10 P.M - 3:30 A.M

GAZ'S ROCKIN BLUES

ST MORITZ

9 Wardour Street

ADM £7... £5 BEFORE 11

10 P.M - 3:30 A.M

THURSDAY OCTOBER 26TH 2006

GAZ'S ROCKIN BLUES

ST MORITZ

9, Wardour St

Soho, London, W.1.

£7... £5 BEFORE 11

10 P.M - 3:30 A.M

THURSDAY NOVEMBER 3 2006

PROUDLY PRESENTING..... FROM BELGIUM: ROCKABILLY AND ROCK'N'ROLL OUTFIT

GAZ'S ROCKIN BLUES

THE **SeatSniffers** LIVE!

★ST MORITZ
159 Wardour Street
ADM £7... £5 BEFORE 11

**THURSDAY
28 SEPT 2006**

PROUDLY PRESENTING....

GAZ'S ROCKIN BLUES

SKAVILL...

ST MORITZ
159, Wardour St
Soho. W.1.
10PM - 3:30AM
ADM £7... £5 BEFORE 11

**THURSDAY 19TH
APRIL 2007**

LIVE!

PROUDLY PRESENTING....

GAZ'S ROCKIN BLUES

ska from brighton

SeCOND TIME LUCKY

LIVE!

ST MORITZ
159, Wardour St
Soho. London. W.1.

ADMISSION £8
£7 BEFORE 11

10PM - 3:30AM

**THURSDAY
12TH JULY 2007**

+ from seattle:
natalie
wouldn't
ska soul rock'n'roll

PROUDLY PRESENTING.....

GAZ'S ROCKIN BLUES

RACI...
WENDY JA...
+ SUPPORT BY...

ST MORITZ
159, Wardour St
Soho. London. W.1.
ADMISSION £8 • £7 BEFORE 11

**THURSDAY
3RD MAY 07**

10P...

GAZ'S ROCKIN BLUES

THURS NOVEMBER 9th 06

LIVE!

ADM £7 come Early
EVERYONE £5 BEFORE 11

ST MORITZ
159, Wardour St
Soho, London, W.1.

CLAY MACHINE GUN

10PM - 3:30AM

PROUDLY PRESENTING.....

GAZ'S ROCKIN BLUES

FROM CORNWALL: TRADITIONAL
CELTIC PUNK-IRISH BAND FOR
A REAL XMAS SHANTY
KNEES-UP

ST MORITZ
159, Wardour St
Soho. London. W.1.
ADM £7... £5 BEFORE 11
10PM - 3:30AM

**THURSDAY 14TH
DECEMBER 2006**

BLACK FRIDAY

GAZ'S ROCKIN BLUES

PROUDLY PRESENTS

GIRLS on TOP
10TH ANNIVERSARY PARTY

LIVE!

ST MORITZ
159, Wardour St
Soho, London. W.1.
ADM £7... £5 BEFORE 11
10PM - 3:30AM

ALSO FEATURING:

JAWBONE
ONE MAN BLUES BAND FROM AMERICA

**THURSDAY 5TH
OCTOBER 2006**

PLUS:
COOL BLUES DUO FROM CAMBRIDGE

PROUDLY PRESENTING.....

GAZ'S ROCKIN BLUES

ska, reggae and
jazzy funk from
Portsmouth

CIRCUS 9...

LONDONS No1 BLUESDANCE

ST MORITZ
159, Wardour St
Soho. London. W.1.
ADM £7... £5 BEFORE 11

**THURSDAY
31ST
MAY 2007**

10P...

GAZ'S ROCKIN BLUES

PROUDLY PRESENTING.....

THE SKAMONIC'

10 P.M - 3:30 A.M

Be SKared
Authentic jazz ska from London t

LIVE!

ST MORITZ
159, Wardour St
Soho, London, W.1.
ADM **£8** ... **£6** BEFORE 11

THURSDAY
17 MAY 07

GAZ'S ROCKIN BLUES

PROUDLY PRESENTING.....

Babylove & tl
VAN DANGOS
rocksteady & ska from denmark

LIVE!

LONDONS Nº 1 BLUESDANCE

ST MORITZ
159, Wardour St
Soho, London, W.1.

ADMISSION **£8** • **£7** BEFORE 11

10 P.M - 3:30 A.M

on
THURS
28 TH JUNE
2007

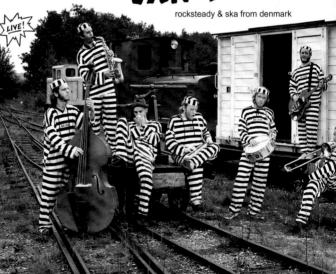

GAZ'S ROCKIN BLUES

ST MORITZ
159, Wardour St
Soho, London, W.1.

ADM·£8... £6 BEFORE 11

THURSDAY

OCTOBER

4TH 2007

Voola

LIVE!

Tight as a Drum

GAZ'S ROCKIN BLUES

ST MORITZ
159, Wardour St
Soho, London, W.1.

ADM·£8... £6 BEFORE 11

THURSDAY

DECEMBER

6TH 2007

soul-fuelled,
dub-induced roots,
rockers & reggae,
featuring members
from the specials,
bentley rhythm ace,
galliano & pwei

LIVE!

GAZ'S ROCKIN BLUES

LONDONS No 1 BLUESDANCE

ST MORITZ
159, Wardour St
Soho, London, W.1

ADM·£8... £6 BEFORE 11

10PM- 3:30AM

**THURSDAY
23 AUGUST
2007**

LIVE!

PROUDLY PRESENTING.....

BOURBON SOAKED
GYPSY BLUES BOP'N'STROLL

The Urban Voodoo Machine

GAZ'S ROCKIN BLUES

★ST MORITZ
159 Wardour Street

ADMISSION £8 · £7 BEFORE 11

10PM- 3:30AM

THURSDAY

16TH AUGUST 2007

PROUDLY PRESENTING ......

HOOLIGAN NIGHT
mutant blues

LIVE!

+ support by

LA CASA BANCALE

from france, a mixture of ska,
rocksteady, reggae, disco,
chanson francaise & gypsy music

10PM- 3:30AM

GAZ'S ROCKIN BLUES

CONTROL THIS

LIVE!

ST MORITZ

59, Wardour St

oho, London, W.1.

ADM·£8. Come Early!
EVERYONE £6 BEFORE 11

10 P.M - 3:30 A.M

HURSDAY

SEPT

20TH 2007

PROUDLY PRESENTING...

HELL'S KITCHEN

on THURS
OCTOBER
25th 2007

AT St MORITZ ADM. £8
159, Wardour St £6
Soho, London, W.1. BEFORE 11 P.M.

LIVE!

10 P.M - 3:30 A.M

GAZ'S ROCKIN BLUES

GHASTLY

LONDONS Nº 1 BLUESDAN

GAZ'S ROCKIN BLUES

★ ST MORITZ
159 Wardour Street

ADM £8... £6 BEFORE 11

10 P.M - 3:30 A.M

THURSDAY
NOVEMBER
8TH 2007

PROUDLY PRESENTS

THE CIRCUS OF SOUND

ska and reggae band
from cornwall

LIVE

GAZ'S ROCKIN BLUES

ST MORITZ
159, Wardour St
Soho, London, W.1.

10 P.M - 3:30 A.M

ADMISSION £8 • £6 BEFORE 11

THURSDAY
NOVEMBER
29TH 2007

The • PROUDLY PRESENTING •

PENETRATORS

rock'n'roll

LIV

GAZ'S ROCKIN BLUES

FEATURING . . .

The Priscillas

rock'n'roll, punk and pop,
balanced with perfectly sweet tunes,
sarky attitude, and romper stomping beats.

ST MORITZ

59 Wardour Street

LIVE!

9 P.M - 3:30 A.M

ADMISSION £8
Come Early!
EVERYONE £6 BEFORE 11

THUR 15TH NOV 2007

PROUDLY PRESENTING.....   ...BRIXTON SKA

GAZ'S ROCKIN BLUES

LIVE!

TOP CATS

St MORITZ
159, Wardour St
Soho, London, W.1.

ADMISSION £8 • £7 BEFORE 11

THURSDAY 4TH JAN 2007

10P.M - 3:30AM

GAZ'S ROCKIN BLUES

LONDONS No1 BLUESDANCE

★ST MORITZ
159 Wardour Street

ADMISSION £8... £6 BEFORE 11

THURSDAY NOVEMBER 1ST 2007

PROUDLY PRESENTS

MADE IN ENGLAND

FEATURING THE SHELLAC SISTERS

THE **SHELLAC COLLECTIVE**

SPEED 78   NO 33/45

GREG'S GREATS 78's

(Pre-Vinyl)

10P.M - 3:50AM

FEATURING...

GAZ'S ROCKIN BLUES

TA-MÈRI

LIVE!

St MORITZ
159, Wardour St
Soho, London

ADMISSION £8
Come Early!
EVERYONE £6 BEFORE 11

10P.M - 3:30AM

THUR 22ND NOV 2007

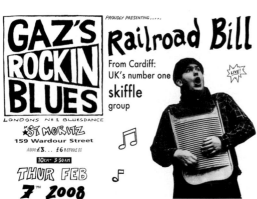

GAZ'S ROCKIN BLUES

LONDONS No1 BLUESDANCE

★ST MORITZ
159 Wardour Street

ADMISSION £8... £6 BEFORE 11

10P.M - 3:50AM

THUR FEB 7TH 2008

PROUDLY PRESENTING.....

Railroad Bill

From Cardiff:
UK's number one
skiffle
group

LIVE!

GAZ'S ROCKIN BLUES

LONDONS Nº 1 BLUESDANCE

★ST MORITZ

159 Wardour Street

ADMISSION £8
£7 BEFORE 11

10P.M - 3:30 A.M

THUR 13 DECEMBER 2007

PROUDLY PRESENTING.....

little Victor
Juke Joint Blues

from the usa

GAZ'S ROCKIN BLUES

ST MORITZ
159, Wardour St
Soho, London, W.1.

ADMISSION £8 • £6 BEFORE 11

10 P.M - 3:30 A.M

THURSDAY
10TH JAN 2008

FEATURING ...

LIVE!

Maybe Myrtle Tyrtle

PROUDLY PRESENTING.....

JACK RABBIT SLIM
SLEAZE-A-BILLY

LIVE!

GAZ'S ROCKIN BLUES

ST MORITZ
Wardour St
, London, W.1.

THURS
FEB 21ST 2008

ADMISSION £8
£7 BEFORE 11
10 P.M - 3:30 A.M

GAZ'S ROCKIN BLUES

ST MORITZ
159, Wardour St
Soho, London, W.1.

ADMISSION £8 ... £6 BEFORE 10

10 P.M - 3:30 A.M

THURSDAY
10TH APRIL
2008

Starring...

THE BOTTLENECKERS + The 5 ACES!
from glasgow

LIVE!

GAZ'S ROCKIN BLUES
LONDONS Nº 1 BLUESDANCE

ST MORITZ
159, Wardour St
Soho, London, W.1.

ADMISSION £8 • £6 BEFORE 11

THURSDAY
MAY 29TH
2008

PROUDLY PRESENTING.....

BIG DANNY
100% authentic rock'n'roll

GAZ'S ROCKIN BLUES

LONDONS N° 1 BLUESDANCE

ST MORITZ
159, Wardour St
Soho, London, W.1.

· PROUDLY PRESENTING ·

DIZ & The DOORMEN!

ADMISSION £8
£7 BEFORE 11

10P.M - 3:30A.M

ON THUR 6TH MAR 2008

PROUDLY PRESENTING..... teenage rock & roll from

GAZ'S ROCKIN BLUES

LONDONS Nº 1 BLUESDANCE

THURS ON 27TH MAR 2008

Kitty, Daisy & Lewis

LIVE!

ST MORITZ
19, Wardour St
Soho, London, W.1.

ADMISSION £8 • £7 BEFORE 11

10 P.M - 3:30 A.M

GAZ'S ROCKIN BLUES

ST MORITZ
59, Wardour St
Soho, London, W.1.

ADM £8... £6 BEFORE 11

10 P.M - 3:30 A.M

THURSDAY 2ND MAY 2008

captain black

GAZ'S ROCKIN BLUES

LONDONS Nº 1 BLUESDANC

PROUDLY PRESENTING.....

LOS SQUIDERO

from way out w
latino rock'n'r
at it's b

★ ST MORITZ
159 Wardour Street

10 P.M - 3:30 A.M

ADM·£8. Come Early!
EVERYONE £6 BEFORE II

THURSDAY
SEPTEMBER 4TH
2008

LIVE!

GAZ'S ROCKIN BLUES

PROUDLY PRESENTING.....

I BLAME COCO

AT ST MORITZ

159 Wardour Street

10 P.M - 3:30 A.M

ADM £8... £6 BEFORE 11

THURSDAY 5TH JUNE 2008

GAZ'S ROCKIN BLUES

MUSIC IS PROVIDED BY...

PENGU!NS

ST MORITZ

159, Wardour St

Soho, London, W.1.

ADM £8, Come Early!

EVERYONE £6 BEFORE 11

10 P.M - 3:30 A.M

THURSDAY 31ST JULY 2008

GAZ'S ROCKIN BLUES

PROUDLY PRESENTING.....

RottenHillGang

Dickensian hip hop crew from Notting Hill

LIVE!

☆ ST MORITZ
159 Wardour Street

ADM £8. Come Early!
EVERYONE £6 BEFORE 11

10 P.M - 3:30 AM

THURS
6TH
NOVEMBER
2008

GAZ'S ROCKIN BLUES

FEATURING...

LIVE!

BRIGHT SIZED GYPSIE

gypsy jazz outfit from birmingham

☆ ST MORITZ
159 Wardour Street

ADMISSION £8 - £6 BEFORE 11

THURSDAY
14TH AUGUST
2008

10 P.M

GAZ'S ROCKIN BLUES

PROUDLY PRESENTING.....

LOS ALBERTOS

swing, jazz, ska, fairground drum and bass from brighton

LIVE!

LONDONS Nº1 BLUESDANCE

☆ ST MORITZ
159, Wardour St
Soho. London. W.1.

ADM £8... £6 BEFORE 11

10 P.M - 3:30 AM

THURSDAY
14TH
MAY 2009

GAZ'S ROCKIN BLUES

PROUDLY PRESENTING.....

THE CRACKL

funky no

LIVE!

LONDONS Nº1 BLUESDANCE

☆ ST MORITZ
159 Wardour Street

10 P.M - 3:30 AM

ADM £8... £6 BEFORE 11

THURSDAY
SEPTEMBER 18TH
2008

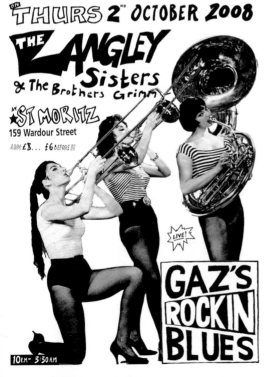

PROUDLY PRESENTING.....

ON THURS 2ND OCTOBER 2008

THE LANGLEY Sisters
& The Brothers Grimm

☆ ST MORITZ
159 Wardour Street

ADM £8... £6 BEFORE 11

LIVE!

GAZ'S ROCKIN BLUES

10 P.M - 3:30 AM

PROUDLY PRESENTING.....

NIK TURNER & HIS BAND

☆ ST MORITZ
159 Wardour Street

ADMISSION £8
£7 BEFORE 11

ON THURS
OCTOBER
16TH
08

GAZ'S ROCKI BL

10 P.M - 3:30 AM

GAZ'S ROCKIN BLUES

THE TROJANS

LIVE!

featuring
rico rodriguez

ST MORITZ
159, Wardour St
Soho, London, W.1.

**ADMISSION £9
£7 BEFORE 11**

10 P.M - 3:30 A.M

A MEMORIAL
IN TRIBUTE TO
DAMIAN KORNER
1957 - 2008

THURSDAY 30ᵀᴴ OCT 08

GAZ'S ROCKIN BLUES

PROUDLY PRESENTING
MICK - ARTISTIK

modern beatnik song s
and crew from

LIV

AT ST MORITZ ADM. £8
159, Wardour St £6
Soho, London, W.1. BEFORE 11 P.M.

10 P.M - 3:30 A.M

THURSDAY
20 NOVEMBER
2008

GAZ'S ROCKIN BLUES

ST MORITZ
159, Wardour St
Soho, London, W.1.

ADMISSION £8
Come Early!
EVERYONE £6 BEFORE 11

10 P.M - 3:30 AM

THURSDAY
5ᵀᴴ FEB
2009

The ORIGINAL
RABBIT FOO
SPASM BA

LIVE

GAZ'S ROCKIN BLUES

ST MORITZ
159, Wardour St
Soho, London, W.1.

ADM £8. Come Early!
EVERYONE £6 BEFORE 11

10 P.M - 3:30 AM

ON THURS
9ᵀᴴ APRIL
2009

PROUDLY PRESENTING.....
THE TOFU LUV
FROGS

LIVE!

GAZ'S ROCKIN BLUES

ST MORITZ
59 Wardour Street

ADM·£8. Come Early!
EVERYONE £6 BEFORE 11

10 P.M – 3:30 A.M

THURSDAY
28 MAY
2009

hammond organ led
funky jazz

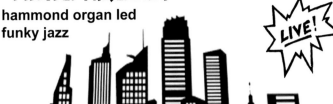

LIVE!

THE FILTHY SIX

GAZ'S ROCKIN BLUES

ST MORITZ
Wardour Street

£8... £6 BEFORE 11

10 P.M – 3:30 A.M

THURSDAY
TH JUNE
2009

PROUDLY PRESENTING.....

SMOKERS
ANGLE SHADES

LIVE!

GAZ'S ROCKIN BLUES

PROUDLY PRESENTS

THE TOO·TONES

LIVE!

THURS
30 TH APRIL
2009

AT ST MORITZ ADM £8
159, Wardour St £6
Soho, London, W.1. BEFORE 11 P.M.

RACEWAY

10 P.M – 3:30 A.M

GAZ'S ROCKIN BLUES

PROUDLY PRESENTING.....

Kingsize Slim

ST MORITZ
159, Wardour St
Soho, London, W.1.

LIVE!

10 P.M - 3:30 A.M

ADMISSION £8
Come Early!
EVERYONE £6 BEFORE 11

THUR
8TH
APRIL
2010

PROUDLY PRESENTING.....

The Delegators

GAZ'S ROCKIN BLUES

LONDONS № 1 BLUESDANCE

ST MORITZ
9 Wardour Street

10 P.M - 3:30 A.M

ADM·£8... £6 BEFORE 11

**THURSDAY
6TH JULY
2009**

LIVE!

RUDE BOY

ROCKSTEADY

PROUDLY PRESENTING.....

Sundowners

rockabilly

LIVE!

GAZ'S ROCKIN BLUES

ST MORITZ
, Wardour St
, London, W.1.

ADM·£8. Come Early!
EVERYONE £6 BEFORE 11

10 P.M - 3:30 A.M

**THURSDAY
OCTOBER
1ST 2009**

PROUDLY PRESENTING.....

GAZ'S ROCKIN BLUES
LONDON

THE ASSASSINS
Mod R&B

LIVE!

AT ST MORITZ   ADM·£8
159, Wardour St   £6
Soho, London, W.1. BEFORE 11 P.M.

**THURSDAY
17 SEPTEMBER
2009**

GAZ'S ROCKIN BLUES

PROUDLY PRESENTING....

SAM the WOMP!

LIVE!

★ST MORITZ
159 Wardour Street

ADMISSION £8 · £6 BEFORE 11

THURS 3RD DEC 2009

10P.M - 3:30 AM

GAZ'S ROCKIN BLUES

PROUDLY PRESENTING.....

BIG T. Lavelle with Raven ISI

RED HOT ROCKIN' BOOGIE BURLESQUE COMBO

★ST MORITZ
159 Wardour Street

ADM £8. Come Early!
EVERYONE £6 BEFORE 11

THURS FEB 18TH 2010

10P.M

GAZ'S ROCKIN BLUES

PROUDLY PRESENTING.....

PRIVATE HAMMONDS ORCHESTRA

THURS 25TH MARCH 2010

from glasgow - MOD r'n'b

LIVE!

ST MORITZ
159, Wardour St
Soho, London, W.1.

ADMISSION £8
Come Early!
EVERYONE £6 BEFORE 11

10P.M - 3:30 AM

GAZ'S ROCKIN BLUES

GIRLS on TOP

LIVE!

★ST MORITZ
159 Wardour Street

10P.M - 3:30 AM
ADM £8... £6 BEFORE 11

THURSDAY 28 JAN 2010

GAZ'S ROCKIN BLUES

· PROUDLY PRESENTING ·

Rude Boy Rasca

brixton rude boy
ska & ting

ST MORITZ
159, Wardour St
Soho, London, W.1.

LIVE!

ADM · £8... £6 BEFORE 11

10P.M - 3:30 AM

THURSDAY 4TH FEB 2010

GAZ'S ROCKIN BLUES

PROUDLY PRESENTS

CRAIG SHAW COMBO

LIVE!

ST MORITZ
59 Wardour Street

10 P.M - 3:30 A.M

ADM·£ 8. Come Early!
EVERYONE £6 BEFORE 11

THUR 21ˢᵗ JAN 2010

PROUDLY PRESENTING.....

THE HIGHTOWN CROWS

GAZ'S ROCKIN BLUES

ST MORITZ
59, Wardour St
ho, London, W.1.

DM·£8... £6 BEFORE 11

10 P.M - 3:30 A.M

HURSDAY
11TH FEB
2010

GAZ'S ROCKIN LUES

ST MORITZ
Wardour Street

PROUDLY PRESENTS

MAMA ROSIN

LIVE!

gypsy swing
from switzerland

THURSDAY
11TH MARCH
2010

ADMISSION £8
Come Early!
EVERYONE £6 BEFORE 11

10 P.M - 3:30 A.M

GAZ'S ROCKIN BLUES

- PROUDLY PRESENTING -

Bogus Gasman

horny
punk
ska

LIVE!

ST MORITZ
159 Wardour Street

ADMISSION £8
Come Early!
EVERYONE £6 BEFORE 11

THURS
1ST
APRIL
2010

10 P.M - 3:30 A.M

GAZ'S ROCKIN BLUES

ST MORITZ
159 Wardour Street

ON THURS 6TH MAY 2010

LIVE!

punky reggae party, the sound of 1976

PROUDLY PRESENTING....

THE ORIGINAL LINE·UP OF

THE MEMBERS

GAZ'S ROCKIN BLUES

THURS 24TH JUNE 2010

ST MORITZ
159 Wardour Street

ADM £9 come Early
EVERYONE £7 BEFORE 11

The Delegators

ska, rocksteady and skinhead reggae

LIVE!

GAZ'S ROCKIN BLUES

LIVE!

ST MORITZ
159, Wardour St
Soho, London. W.1.

ADM £8 ... £6 BEFORE 00

THURSDAY 20 MAY 2010

PROUDLY PRESENTS

FOGHORN LEGHORN

GAZ'S ROCKIN BLUES

PROUDLY PRESENTING....

Kingsize Slim!

ST MORITZ
159, Wardour St
Soho, London. W.1.

LIVE!

10 P.M - 3:30 AM

ADMISSION £8
Come Early!
EVERYONE £6 BEFORE 11

THUR 8TH APRIL 2010

GAZ'S ROCKIN BLUES

LONDONS No 1 BL

PROUDLY PRESENTING....

JACK RABBIT SLIM

SLEAZE A BILLY

ST MORITZ
159, Wardour St
Soho, London. W.1.

ON THURS 13 MAY 2010

ADMISSION £7 BEF

10 P.M -

GAZ'S ROCKIN BLUES

RÄFVEN

LIVE!

ST MORITZ

59 Wardour Street

M·£8... £7 BEFORE 11

THURS 17 JUNE 2010

10 P.M - 3:30 A.M

PROUDLY PRESENTS

ITTY, DAISY & LEWIS ♫

LIVE!

3:30 A.M

GAZ'S ROCKIN BLUES

★ ST MORITZ

159 Wardour Street

30th anniversary

PARTY special

ADMISSION £9 • £8 BEFORE 11

ON THURS 1st JULY 2010

GAZ'S ROCKIN BLUES

30th anniversary

featuring THE TROJANS
live at 10pm

at THE COBDEN CLUB
170 Kensal Road
London W10 5BN
www.thecobden.co.uk

Saturday
3rd July
2010
7pm-3am

J's

GAZ MAYALL
NATTY BO
BABY SOUL
+ TOMMY DIAMOND
COUNT CASAVUBU

ɔm-10pm

preview with readings
of forthcoming book
GAZ'S ROCKIN' BLUES –
THE FIRST 30 YEARS
on trolleybooks

free entry
before 10pm
£5 after for
non-members

W10

SVP ESSENTIAL:
llamyburrows@yahoo.co.uk
bin@thecobden.co.uk
ail@elinorfahrman.com

"IF ANYONE'S INTERESTED, I WILL BE AT GAZ'S ROCKIN' BLUES STAGE, THE BEST PLACE TO BE."

MATTHEW WRIGHT, THE WRIGHT STUFF, TV SHOW, RE: NOTTING HILL CARNIVAL 2009

CARNIVAL

I tried not to miss any Thursday nights. I did a job for Chris Blackwell for the 40th anniversary of Island records in '97 where I travelled to Japan, Germany, New York and LA, producing Ska Island, which featured Prince Buster, The Skatalites and Fishbone. Released that summer, it turned out to be the last album Chris put out before he sold the company. During the whole project I managed not to miss a single Thursday. I still get to Japan once or twice a year, plus a week at Glastonbury festival, where I now have my own marquee, but apart from that you can expect to see me down the club each week.

I've been running a sound system at Notting Hill Carnival with my brother Jason since the early 90's, outside The Globe on Talbot Road. We'd known the owner, Roy Stewart, for donkey's years. A local unsung hero from Jamaica, he'd set up his restaurant and basement club in the 60's. He was a key figure in restoring calm and easing racial tensions during the Notting Hill race riots in the late 50's, when he had a muscle-building gym around the corner in Powis Square. Jason helped revive the place in the late 80's when he ran it for a few years. By the time the police and council took more control of the carnival in the 90's, drastically reducing the number of sound systems, we'd secured our pitch. With a different fancy dress theme each year we expanded our spot to the point where today we're the biggest, as well as the best-dressed site at carnival. It serves as a great window display of all that Gaz's Rockin' Blues represents and aspires to, and has become the biggest event in my annual calendar. Extremely popular, it helps introduce new generations of young people to the club. It's an integral part of the club story and lots of key players in the team who build and create our set are club regulars; actress Emma Malin, Mutoid Waste Company artists Joe Rush, Sam Haggerty and Dynamite Dave, and all the Smash crew from Jason's yard under the Westway where we prepare the props. Canadian born artist Gordon McHarg aka 'King of the Cut Outs' has been a major help since the beginning, as has Gary Chapman when he's back from film work in LA. Clash bassman and artist, Paul Simonon, has contributed with a couple of great backdrops, as has Natty Bo, Donna Maclean and other great local artists.

One of the club's most important contributors in the last decade has been Baby Soul. Like Natty, she's a great DJ and a superb artist. Whatever they touch turns to gold. She's a fundamental part of our current scene and for the past seven years she's done most of the flyers. Unlike the cut, stick and paste, Tipp-Ex days of the 80's and 90's she's vastly improved the standard of the poster art with a little help from a computer, scanner and some of my graphics. She's also been a prime creative force in our carnival décor, producing some amazing 40ft long backdrops amongst other superb pieces. She regularly DJs at the club these days, adding a touch of sex-appeal to the music, ever since Grainne Kearney, our majorly hot girl DJ, moved to start her own nights elsewhere.

In order for a club to remain successful, I truly believe it must embrace everybody; I encourage all ages. We still have, on occasion, elderly statesmen of music, like Rico, Tan Tan, Duke Vin, Rudy and Groker grace the place. But by and large it's a young people's domain. It appeals to all those young at heart and can keep one feeling young. It's had a Dorian Gray effect on me. When the smoking ban came into force in 2007 it did little to diminish the atmosphere. It just forced a big chunk of the party-goers out on to the street, adding to the sometimes lengthy queues outside. People have often asked me why don't I move to a bigger club? Who knows about the future, but for now I couldn't be happier than I am with the way it is. The majority of the people filling the club now weren't even born when I started this; the parents of many of these kids were regulars of the club when they were of the same age. It's got to be one of the few places where the kids can arrive with their parents without embarrassment. Guest DJs, Aaron and Brillo Pad - The Ram Jam Brothers, often bring their dad along when they come to play and I've seen Lily with her dad Keith Allen there more than once.

It's nice that famous stars of stage and screen can come down without fear of harassment. Some big name faces may not be used to such crammed intimacy, so it's my job as host to ease the way and make people feel welcome. I tend not to make a fuss but must admit that when Scarlett Johansson and Natalie Portman turned up I did buy them a bottle of champagne and led them to a good table near the dance floor. It was so loud though I didn't stop and chat, but they seemed to be having a great time.

I still do my compilations, though no longer on vinyl or tapes. I did a couple for Trojan Records, which got me lots of publicity, coinciding with the time when the club was really taking off again. I'm sure they gave an extra boost when they hit the market culminating with my Club Classics, promoting my 25th anniversary. The same year the Ace compilation I'd done in 1981 was released on CD for the first time. I got to go into their vaults and select a few new tracks for it of obscure, never released before material.

My 30th anniversary celebrations included a tour to Japan with The Skatalites, an exhibition of the club's poster art at the Subway Gallery in Edgware Road, my stage at the Rocket Lounge in Shangri-La at Glastonbury and Notting Hill Carnival, plus a couple of other showcases around town throughout the summer. Aside from that you can be pretty sure to find me DJing, singing and partying every Thursday at Gaz's Rockin' Blues in Soho. It's home from home and I love it as much now as I ever did.

Thirty years well spent and looking forward to many more parties.

left - right:
Natty Bo, Gaz and
Tommy Diamond,
2003

A BIG SHOUT TO ALL THE PEOPLE WHO HAVE
CONTRIBUTED TO THIS BOOK, INCLUDING PHOTOGRAPHERS
PHOENIX J BAY, EVA EDSJÖ, YASU, NICK PALLISER AND ALL
THE WONDERFUL ARTISTS, MANY WHO'VE ALREADY BEEN
MENTIONED, AND OF COURSE A MASSIVE BIG UP TO
EVERYONE WHO'S EVER COME TO GAZ'S ROCKIN' BLUES.

Natty Bo, 2008

Baby Soul and
Tommy Diamond,
2008

Vin Gordon with
The Trojans, 2009

Shane MacGowan,
left, 2004

Gaz and Daisy
Durham, 2009

Masato and Kimi,
2010

Fatman and Gaz at
St Moritz, 2010

Natty on the floor,
2010

Queuing outside St
Moritz on a
Thursday night,
2010

CLUB

Established 1960

159

OJ and Roger
at the door, 2010

Baby Soul, 2009

Gaz outside the
entrance to St
Moritz, 2010

Gaz's Family, 1979
left - right
Josh, Pamela,
Tom, Geoff Wynn,
Ivy the dog, Red,
Ben, Jason and
Gaz Mayall.
Photo by Mark
Lebon

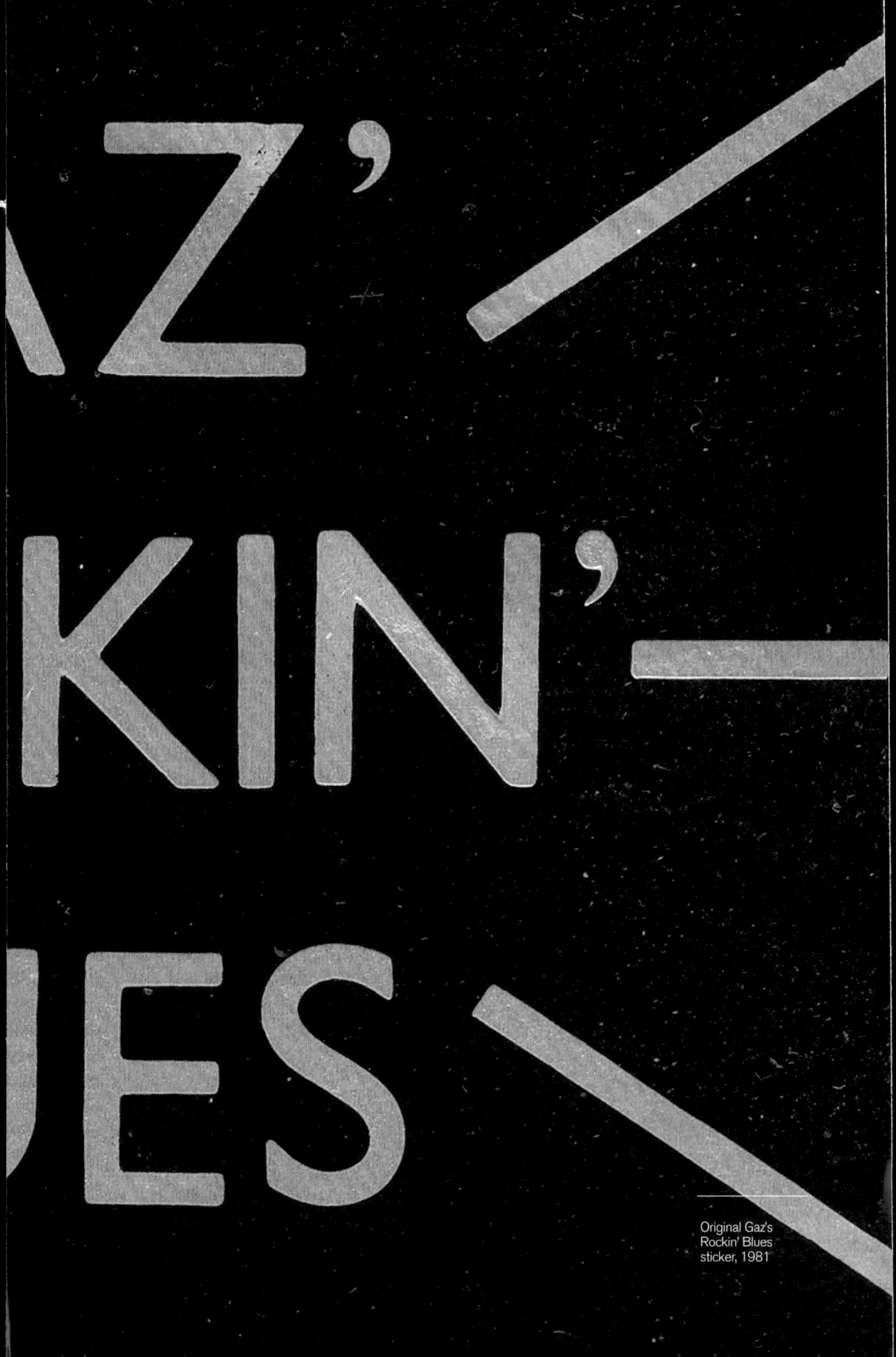

AZ'

KIN' —

JES

Original Gaz's
Rockin' Blues
sticker, 1981

Published in Great Britain
in 2010 by Trolley Ltd
www.trolleybooks.com

Texts©Gaz Mayall, 2010
Photographs©Phoenix J Bay,
Eva Edsjö, Yasu, Nick Palliser, Mark Lebon
Flyers artwork: Christian Coral, Andrew Crawford,
Hans, Gaz Mayall, Elinor Fahrman
Commissioning editor: Elinor Fahrman
Creative Direction: Gigi Giannuzzi
Design & Art Direction: Nathan Dytor
Text Editing:Elinor Fahrman,Hannah Watson,
Grace Pilkington

A catalogue record for this book is available
from the British Library.

ISBN 978-1-907112-15-7

Printed in Italy 2010 by Grafiche Antiga